DOMESTIC INFLUENCES ON SOVIET FOREIGN POLICY

Dina Rome Spechler

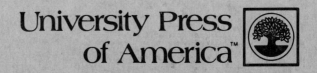
University Press of America™

DOMESTIC INFLUENCES ON SOVIET FOREIGN POLICY

Dina Rome Spechler

Withdrawn

University Press of America

Library of Congress Catalog Card Number: 78-61396

ACKNOWLEDGEMENTS

I should like to express my gratitude to the Soviet and East European Research Centre of Hebrew University and the Leonard Davis Institute for International Relations, also of Hebrew University, for their joint sponsorship of my research on this study.

I should also like to thank my assistants, Ida Isaac and Ruth Yanai-Streseman, for their cheerful and diligent help in the research and preparation of the manuscript. I am grateful, too, to Professors William Zimmerman, James Kurth, Michael Mandelbaum and Philip Gillette, who took the time to read and comment on various drafts of this work. Special thanks are due to Dr. Galia Golan, who first suggested that I undertake a work of this nature and whose interest and comments were invaluable to me in executing it. Finally, I should like to thank my parents, Sydney and Beatrice Rome, and my husband, Martin, for their unfailing support and encouragement, without which this work could never have been completed.

TABLE OF CONTENTS

ABOUT THE AUTHOR

Dina Spechler received a B.A. in Social Studies
from Radcliffe College and a Ph.D. in Government from
Harvard University. She was a Lecturer in the Department of Government of Harvard University and a member
of the Harvard University Russian Research Center.
She is presently in the Department of Political Science
of Tel Aviv University, where she teaches Soviet politics
and international relations. She is the author of articles
on the politics of U.S.-Soviet trade, Soviet nationality
policy, the Soviet Union and the oil weapon, and Soviet
policy toward the Middle East. She is now completing
a book on permitted dissent in the U.S.S.R.

I.

INTRODUCTION

Almost from the founding of the Soviet state, scholars have sought to determine the sources of its conduct in world affairs. The emergence of the USSR as a major world power after the Second World War only lent that effort a new urgency and significance. Recent Soviet interest in detente and the possibility of reducing international tensions through Soviet-American accommodation has made it even more important that we in the West understand what lies behind Soviet foreign policy behavior. This is especially true of Soviet policy in the Middle East, an area in which Soviet-American cooperation is imperative if world peace is to be preserved.

The majority of those who have analyzed Soviet policy in the Middle East have focused on the intentions of the USSR and its leaders in this region. The methods used to ascertain those intentions have differed. A number of writers have attempted to establish the interests or goals of the USSR in the Middle East on the basis of what they postulate to be the general goals of Soviet foreign policy and policy-makers as a group.[1] Others have tried to elicit information about Soviet aims from the statements of Soviet leaders and other materials in the Soviet press.[2] Some have inferred Soviet purposes from Soviet actions.[3] Many have made use of a combination of these methods. But while their techniques for determining Soviet goals have varied, most scholars have employed the same explanatory procedure. They have tried to show how the behavior of the USSR has followed from its global and regional objectives. They have, in other words, sought to demonstrate the logic of Soviet conduct in the Middle East.

1

Much less work has been done on the forces and factors which effect the formulation and attainment of Soviet objectives in this area of the world. this is particularly true of internal forces and factors. Some writers have analyzed the military and economic needs and capabilities of the USSR in order to elucidate Soviet stakes in the Middle East and the constraints on Soviet policy there.[4] The economic studies do shed light on the relationship between domestic resources and requirements and foreign behavior. But there has been very little investigation of what one might call the internal influences on or inputs into the policy process with respect to the Middle East. One writer, having broadly sketched the major internal influences on Soviet foreign policy in general, has briefly applied his analysis to the Middle East.[5] Accounts of Soviet perceptions of the Third World, including the Middle East, imply that ideological formulations and changes in those formulations have had an impact on the shaping of policy.[6] There has been some discussion of the rise of Soviet interest in the developing countries, Middle Eastern and other, as the consequence of changes in the ruling personalities in the USSR.[7] And there have been a few studies of the politics of policy-making, focusing on the opinions on Middle East policy voiced in politically influential circles.[8] But this approach has not been widely used. The internal factors important in the shaping of Soviet Middle Eastern policy, especially elite opinions on the subject, have been relatively neglected (as have internal constraints on the elite attitudes toward Soviet foreign policy generally[9]).

There are a number of reasons for this neglect. One obstacle to research on internal influences on Soviet foreign policy is the persistence, largely at an unconscious level, of the belief that internal constraints are not very important in the Soviet system. This belief was initially generated by the once widely accepted view that the USSR was a totalitarian society and hence one in which there were few significant societal inputs into the policy process. Adherents of this view assumed that totalitarian leaders

2

are free from most or all of the pressures and limitations to which decision-makers in less authoritarian and less controlled societies are subject. Since nearly all of the society's resources were at their disposal, mobilizing those resources and directing them to their foreign policy ends were thought to be a relatively easy task. Totalitarian rulers did not need to worry about attracting voters, raising campaign funds, or defeating rival candidates. They did not have to mollify an independent press or elicit cooperation from independent segments of the government. Thus, it was assumed, they could disregard or readily manipulate the opinions and desires of the population as a whole and even of elite groups within it. Even ideology was generally viewed more as an instrument of power, shaped and molded to suit the needs of those in power, than as a constraint on foreign policy.[10]

Since the beginning of the 1960's, the totalitarian model has been much attacked, and it is often urged that it be abandoned as a basis for studying Soviet domestic politics in the post-Stalin era.[11] Yet this model and the image of Soviet politics which it projects have retained a hold on the minds of many of those who analyze Soviet external behavior.[12] This in part accounts for the relative lack of attention to internal influences on that behavior.

Yet even scholars who are persuaded that foreign policy is very much influenced by internal factors have not written a great deal about them. One important reason for this is the difficulty of obtaining information about those factors. This is particularly true with regard to elite opinions and their impact on policy. Even during Khrushchev's rule, a period which has come to be regarded as the heyday of post-Stalin debate on policy questions, conflicts over foreign policy were never as fully exposed to view as disagreements on internal issues.[13] In recent years there has been a marked decline of public debate in nearly all areas,[14] and it has certainly not become easier to find evidence of differences of opinion on foreign policy.

Yet some evidence is available. Some differences do manifest themselves in the Soviet media. The chief obstacle to research on elite conflict on foreign policy is the difficulty of interpreting the differences one does find. One frequently observes various organs of the press using quite distinct, characteristic phrases and formulations when they discuss the same foreign policy issue. But these are expressed in highly veiled, sometimes esoteric, language and often quite laconic formulas, which are capable of being interpreted in a number of different ways. In October, 1973, for example, one major newspaper, *Sovetskaya Rossiya*, describes Israel as "as agent of international imperialism, a link in the chain of imperialist policy."[15] Another newspaper, *Pravda*, avers that Israel "has been enjoying the support and protection of imperialist circles" and charges that "foreign reactionary circles" "share responsibility for the current development of events in the Near East."[16] A third, *Izvestiya*, insists "Israel *alone* is responsible for her acts."[17] Do the first two publications wish to blame the United States for the outbreak of war in the Middle East, but the third to absolve it? Is the first suggesting a larger American role than the second? Can one say that *Sovetskaya Rossiya* regards Israel as a mere puppet or pawn in the hands of larger forces, while *Pravda* views it as a partner, if not initiator? Or do the differences in wording reflect no underlying disagreement?[18] There is no sure way to know. At best one can only seek larger patterns to which these individual instances seem to conform.

The task of interpretation is made all the more difficult by the fact that there is rarely a genuine exchange of views. Organs of the press do not usually attack one another's positions on foreign policy questions. Often what constitutes "debate" is the assertion of an opinion by one individual or newspaper and failure on the part of others even to discuss the issue. Detente "creates favorable possibilities for the national liberation movement," says *Pravda*.[19] *Komsomolskaya Pravda* discusses both detente and the national liberation movement, but pointedly refrains from linking the two. *Pravda* extols the

4

socialist character of Russia's Middle Eastern allies;[20] *Komsomol-skaya Pravda* does not print these complimentary remarks.

Another problem that arises with materials of this nature is that of determining whether different formulations are the result of divergent opinions, or whether they are intentionally created and coordinated by a single source.[21] Reports by Westerners who have closely observed the Soviet media and by emigres who have worked in them suggest that when there is orchestration, there is uniformity; differences are manifested only when there is lack of direction or defiance or direction.[22] Moreover, it is known that Communist leaders strongly prefer to display a united front to the West whenever possible.[23] They believe that in unity there is strength, in division weakness.[24] Thus one could assume that they would generally avoid revealing their differences and would certainly not give the appearance of divergent views when they do not exist. However, even if this is the general policy, there might be exceptions to the rule. This aspect of the Soviets' "operational code"[25] might sometimes be violated. There is room for uncertainty in any specific instance.[26]

An equally perplexing difficulty which arises in any effort to study divergent opinions as possible influences on the policy process is that even if we have reason to believe that verbal differences do reflect actual differences of opinion, we can never know with great assurance whose opinions a speaker or writer represents. On a number of occasions *Pravda* and *Izvestiya* distinguish themselves from the other major Soviet newspapers by calling for the liberation of specifically those lands which were occupied by Israel in 1967.[27] (The more common, intentionally vague formula demands Israeli withdrawal from "the occupied Arab territories.") The question is, whose position are *Pravda* and *Izvestiya* articulating? Is this merely the stand two individual staff members want the regime to take? Is it the view of the editors of the two newspapers? Does it reflect the thinking of some important officials, and if so, which ones? Is there a sizeable group of people who hold this view? How powerful is this group? One cannot ultimately assess the political importance of divergent opinions unless one knows whose opinions they are, how large a part in the policy process is played by those who hold them, and how much political weight or leverage they possess.

Finally there is the problem that the kind of debate one encounters in the Soviet press on foreign policy issues rarely includes defense of concrete policy proposals or endorsement (even veiled) of specific actions. Instead, what one usually finds are statements of general goals, opinions about a situation or state of affairs, or comments on a foreign country, leader or political group and its policies or behavior. One cannot automatically assume that praise of measures taken by non-Soviet actors implies advocacy that the same steps be taken by the USSR. Thus the all-important inference from general opinions expressed to courses of action which are favored by various elite groups is one the analyst must make without much hard evidence.

But when all this has been said, all these reservations registered, in this author's view, the investigation of elite opinions through analysis of the Soviet media is still worth undertaking. Too little has been done for us to be certain that it will prove unprofitable. Only if we attempt the task can we really know whether the relative scarcity, opacity and ambiguity of the materials render it truely infeasible. The problems involved give us reason to be guarded in reaching conclusions, but not (at this stage) to abandon the effort altogether.

It is no longer possible to assume that Soviet foreign affairs are directed by a single mind, operating in isolation from and without regard for the opinions of others in high positions. There is too much evidence that policy-making in the USSR involves conflict and compromise for such models of Soviet decision-making to have much plausibility.[28] Nor can one assume that those who participate in the foreign policy decision process represent only themselves, that they are in no way and at no time spokemen for institutions, groups and likeminded colleagues. In a highly bureaucratized society like the Soviet Union, it would be most surprising if individual decision-makers did not often act as defenders of organizational interests and views.[29] Indeed, elite group representation has been frequently observed in the domestic policy process.[30] While less is known about how foreign policy decisions are made, group influence on the foreign policy process has been noted.[31] Moreover, studies of other political systems suggest that major differences in the nature of the policy process arise not as one moves from the domestic to the foreign sphere, but from one type of issue-area to another.[32] Thus the abundant evidence of the influence of elite groups on the making of Soviet internal policy gives us reason to expect that such groups also have a substantial impact on the shaping of foreign policy. This makes the study of elite opinions on external affairs both worthwhile and important.

At the same time, the dearth of information about the foreign policy process indicates that such research is needed to extend our understanding of the Soviet political process in general. The very paucity of systematic studies has tended to encourage speculation about groups and factions affecting fo[reign policy decision-making. It would be desirable to obtain even meagre evidence which would confirm popular assumptions or point out the direction in which they should be modified. For that matter, the very failure of a systematic study to detect the divisions often assumed to exist would be significant. It should encourage us to reformulate our hypotheses as to the issues about whoch conflict exists and the lineup in the battle. If it proves fruitful, such an investigation can also advance the study of comparative foreign policy, enabling us to compare and contrast domestic sources of foreign policy in one- and multi-party states and in socialist and capitalist social systems.

With these considerations in mind, this author undertook to study elite opinions on Soviet policy in the Middle East during the period of the October, 1973 war. The decision to concentrate on the Middle East was made for a number of reasons. One of these was stated at the outset: given the persistence of extreme tension in the area and the high levels of Soviet and American involvement there, it seemed particularly important and urgent to understand the forces impinging on Soviet policy in this region. Secondly, this area promised to be a fruitful one for research on internal influences on foreign policy. An analysis of studies of domestic policy seemed to indicate that elite groups most often participate in and have an impact on the Soviet policy process in two kinds of cases: situations in which there are substantial resources to be allocated and situations in which the role, authority or prestige of powerful institutions is at stake. Both these elements are present in Soviet policy in the Middle East. Soviet involvement there has entailed large and continually increasing expenditures and has both posed a threat and created opportunities for powerful domestic groups and factions. Thus there was strong reason to think that elite groups might have been active and influential in the making of Middle Eastern policy. Moreover, the little that was known of Soviet decision-making on this subject from those who had some opportunity to observe the process at close hand, and who themselves tried to influence it, suggested that a fair number (if not all) of the top leaders were involved in it and that there was considerable disagreement among them.[33] This inference was supported by the findings of Dimant-Kass,[34] whose work also encouraged the author to think that research in this area might yield interesting results.[35]

The choice of the period of time to be studied was dictated by a number of considerations. The author's original intention had been to study the impact of the October events on internal policy debate in the year after the war. However, some preliminary investigation persuaded her to concentrate her study on the period of the war itself. In the first place, it was impossible to discern the effect of the war on elite opinion without knowing more about elite attitudes and disagreements prior to and during the war. Secondly, it quickly became

8

apparent that it would be easier to study differences of opinion during the war than during the months which followed it. The coverage of the Middle East in the Soviet press was much more intensive while there was fighting in the region than after the cease-fire became effective. While it lasted, the war occupied the attention of every major newspaper and was at least touched upon by nearly every major speech and every important figure who spoke. This was a rare opportunity to look for variations in attitudes, expressed within reasonable time proximity of one another. (Long time lags sometimes make it difficult to know whether observed differences of opinion reflect different attitudes on the part of two speakers or newspapers, or simply a general shift in attitude over the course of the time period.) The fact that during the war specific events and episodes elicidated comment from all media sources meant that one could make detailed comparisons of the articles appearing in various organs and look for subtle nuances in the treatment each gave the same topic.

The period of the war recommended itself for other reasons. It was a time when major decisions had to be made: should the Soviets try to restrain their clients? should they aid them? what kind of aid should be given, and what conditions should be attached to it? should the Soviets encourage or oppose efforts to obtain a cease-fire? should they promote the use of the oil embargo? These were only a few of the items which must have been on the wartime agenda of the Politburo. These were matters of tremendous importance, which affected Soviet interests in nearly every area of the globe: their relationship with the United States, the strategic balance between the U.S. and the USSR, the Soviet image in the Third World, Soviet credibility in Eastern Europe and the preparedness of the Warsaw Pact forces. The sums involved were large, the political and military stakes high. Surely many high officials and powerful groups would want tp affect the decision process, and surely thier interests and their stands would not be identical.

In general the impact of elite groups and, indeed, their

9

ability to function, tends to be greatest when there is an active struggle for power underway. The activity of these groups is most likely to be encouraged or tolerated in one of two situations: when no individual has achieved clear dominance in the top leadership and one or more of its members are trying to do so;[36] or when one individual has attained such a position and is actively attempting to consolidate his power.[37] Under such circumstances, the chief contenders in the struggle need the support of influential elites and will be most likely to allow them to voice their opinions. The elites themselves have the greatest incentive to speak out. They have an opportunity both to influence the outcome of the struggle and to place the contenders in their debt by extending them the support they need.

In October, 1973, the second type of situation existed in the USSR. A few months before, Brezhnev had made the second of the two major bids for power which he had attempted since he succeeded Khrushchev as head of the Party. The first of these, in April, 1971, had resulted in a clear victory for the Secretary General. Four men with close professional ties to Brezhnev and generally beleived to be his protégés, were granted Politburo membership.[38] But Brezhnev's second attempt to strengthen his own position within the ruling group was not so unambiguously successful. In April, 1973, Brezhnev engineered the removal of an important rival, Shelest, and a major critic of the Secretary General, Voronov. Voronov had only four months before been appointed the head of a newly formed special committee to reappraise Soviet relations with Egypt, in the wake of unrest in Cairo over Egyptian policy in the Middle East. He was known to be a policy-maker in this area, and his removal could well have been the result of disagreement with Brezhnev on Middle East questions. At this time Brezhnev brought onto the Politburo the Foreign Minister, Andrei Gromyko, an ardent supporter (if not chief architect) of his detente policy. But two other men also became Politburo members at that time, Defense Minister Grechko and KGB head Andropov. While both of these individuals had warm personal associations with Brezhnev, both were powerful figures in their own right, and both had expressed reservations about Brezhnev's foreign policy.[39] These developments suggested that when the October war broke out, a high-level struggle over power and policy was probably still underway, with foreign policy, quite possibly Soviet Middle Eastern policy, a central issue. This, in turn, made it very likely that elite groups with distinct and probably contradictory positions on Middle East policy would be active and vocal during the war, when so many crucial foreign policy decisions had to be made.

II.

THE ISSUES,
SOURCES AND ASSUMPTIONS

One of the most eminent interpreters of Soviet politics, Zbigniew Brzezinski, has pointed out that the Soviets do not treat issues of foreign folicy as discrete problems, to be dealt with independently, in isolation from one another and the larger political and historical context in which they arise.[40] It was accordingly assumed in this study that if specific moves or tactics to be employed during the war were a subject of discussion and argument, it was likely that there was also debate on the larger policy context in which these problems were embedded. The author thus looked for differences of opinion on the following sets of issues:

1) Immediate action. (What should the USSR do now that hostilities have broken out?)
2) Analysis of the immediate situation.
   a) How is the USSR affected by the outbreak of hostilities?
   b) Why did hostilities break out? Who is responsible?
3) Soviet foreign policy goals in general.
   a) What general objectives should Soviet Middle Eastern policy serve?
   b) What extra- or supra-regional considerations should be kept in mind in the formulation of Middle Eastern policy?
4) Future Soviet policy in the Middle East.
   a) Should the USSR be involved there? Why?
   b) What should the USSR work for in the Middle East? How should it work for these things?

    c) Whom should the USSR support in the Middle East? Whom should it oppose?

    d) What political and military objectives of its Middle Eastern clients should be supported? Which should be opposed?

    e) What tactics should the USSR promote?

    f) What should be the nature and scope of Soviet aid in the area?

  5) Global forces and developments likely to further or impede Soviet policy in the Middle East.

The author based her research on six major Soviet newspapers, selected for their importance, as measured by "circulation" or number of copies printed; for their history of expressing distinctive political outlooks or "tendencies of articulation;"[41] and for their probable links with influential elite groups. It was not assumed that any one newspaper reflected the views of an entire functional group or institution. One cannot expect unity of opinion within any profession or organization unless the issue would directly affect the interests of all members and affect them all in the same way. Few issues are of this sort,[42] and Soviet Middle Eastern policy is certainly not one of them. One might anticipate considerable differences of opinion on this subject within the military, for example, for the costs and benefits of Soviet involvement in the area must be calculated quite differently by the navy, the tactical air force and ground forces.[43] The same is surely true of industrial managers, some of whom would benefit from the USSR's commitments to its clients there, and others of whom would lose (or would gain more from a different kind of involvement). There must be many Party officials whose personal interests are not affected in any obvious way, and whose views in so complex a policy area are therefore divergent.

However, it was assumed that each newspaper did speak for at least one influential individual or elite group. Each paper selected reaches many thousands of readers. It is very likely that political elites would be anxious to use each of them to

14

express their opinions. It is also likely that Politburo members would want to control them, to shape their treatment of the news in accordance with their own views, and to appoint as editors individuals who would do that for them. Thus it is safe to assume that the opinions expressed in the pages of these papers would be those of powerful groups or individuals, probably (although not necessarily) including Politburo members.

The six papers selected were *Pravda, Izvestiya, Krasnaya Zvezda, Sovetskaya Rossiya, Komsomolskaya Pravda* and *Trud.* The selection of *Pravda,* the chief organ of the Party Central Committee, was based on the observation that for several years it had fairly faithfully reflected the views of Secretary General Brezhnev and his supporters within the Party apparatus. The author assumed that, as typically had been the case in the past, state and economic officials would use *Izvestiya,* an organ of the Council of Ministers, as an outlet for their views, and that its general policy line would conform to that of the Chairman of the Council, Kosygin. A link had been observed between *Krasnaya Zvezda,* the newspaper of the Defense Ministry, and Defense Minister Grechko, and it was assumed that this paper spoke both for him and for an influential segment of the military.[44] *Sovetskaya Rossiya,* the newspaper published by the Russian Republic Council of Ministers, was studied because it had consistently been a voice of Russian nationalism. (It had been associated with Polyansky, Politburo member and Minister of Agriculture during the October war.) The author chose *Komsomolskaya Pravda,* the paper of the Komsomol organization, as a frequent mouthpiece for establishment ideologues (the promoters and expounders of ideology and defenders of ideological orthodoxy in the ranks of the Komsomol, the Party apparatus and the KGB). It is widely assumed that at the time of the October War, Politburo member Suslov was associated with this group. The Trade Union organ, *Trud,* had generally reflected the opinions of Shelepin, the head of that organization, and of his supporters in the KGB and Komsomol, who could be expected to oppose Brezhnev on both ideological and opportunistic grounds.[45]

The author describes the clusters of individuals who share the opinions expressed by these newspapers as "opinion groups." The requirement for "groupness" is simply a shared outlook. Quite probably these opinion groups also met other criteria often specified for the use of the concept of "group," such as member interaction, mutual awareness of shared views, and a stable core of members.

III.

THE FINDINGS

1.

As might have been predicted from its association with Brezhnev, detente is *Pravda's* primary preoccupation in the foreign policy sphere during the period of the October war. In this paper's view detente is clearly the USSR's most important policy objective, and *Pravda* very often discusses the situation in the Middle East in connection with it. Apparently Soviet critics of detente seized on the war as an occasion to voice their reservations or opposition to this policy. Brezhnev and his supporters were obviously concerned to defend detente to its internal opponents, to show them that it served, rather than impeded, the interests both of the USSR's clients in the Middle East and of the Soviet Union itself. True, *Pravda* concedes, the events in the Middle East demonstrate "how complicated and difficult is the struggle for peace, security and cooperation among peoples, how much effort it demands." "But", it continues, "this is the sole correct course, which serves the interests of all peoples."[46] To domestic critics who complain that the interests of Arab socialism and the national liberation movement in the Middle East are being sacrificed to detente, *Pravda* answers: quite the contrary. Who could speak more authoritatively on the subject than the Arab Communist and workers' parties themselves? *Pravda* alone, of all the major Soviet papers, quotes from a resolution adopted by a conference of representatives of Communist and workers' parties of the Arab states, held in September, 1973. The conference, according to *Pravda*, thanked Brezhnev for his efforts for world

17

peace. It commended his initiative in visiting the United States in June, 1973, and praised the intensification of detente which resulted from it, for "'this [policy] is creating more favorable possibilities for the Arab national liberation movement.'"[47]

Pravda actually uses the war as a case in point to show Soviet opponents of detente that it has served a useful purpose, in moderating U.S. policy. This paper portrays American policy in the Middle East as reasonable and restrained, and not inimical to the aims of the USSR in the area or to the goals of its Arab friends. For example, it carries a report of a *Christian Science Monitor* article purportedly asserting that the United States is not committed to help Israel seize the Arab lands it seized in the 1967 war.[48] *Pravda* quotes Kissinger as saying that the U.S. wants hostilities to be ended in a manner which would contribute to the maximum extent possible to the promotion of a permanent solution to the Middle East conflict.[49] (Apparently this Kissinger formula meant the Arabs must be allowed to emerge from the war with some territorial gains. Surely not even Soviet hawks would object.)

With the outbreak of hostilities Brezhnev had to contend with a probable increase in external, as well as internal, opposition to detente. Thus we find *Pravda* making great efforts to reassure American skeptics, who might interpret the war as a demonstration of Soviet willingness to discard this policy in favor of other foreign policy goals. *Pravda* constantly stresses the importance of detente to the USSR and repeatedly reaffirms Soviet commitment to it.[50] It takes pains to show that the USSR has not violated the spirit of detente by encouraging unprovoked aggression. The Soviets' Middle Eastern allies are moderate and peace-loving.[51] They have continually sought a non-violent solution to the Middle East conflict. It is Israel, not the Soviets' clients, who has repeatedly sabotaged all efforts to achieve such a solution, and who is therefore responsible for the outbreak of war.[52] Like Brezhnev in his speeches, *Pravda* generally avoids criticizing the United States. The other newspapers reprint Arab condemnations of the United States; *Pravda* does not.[53]

While the Party newspaper does implicate the United States in the war, accusing it of supporting Israeli intransigence and aggression, it does not follow the rest of the media in depicting Israel as a mere puppet or agent of American imperialism.[54] Whatever the other results of the fighting may be, *Pravda* wants to make sure that it leaves detente intact.

Pravda has two other objectives which are at least of equal importance and of even greater urgency now that hostilities have broken out. The first is to insure that the Soviet Union does not lose its foothold in the Middle East. *Pravda's* (and Brezhnev's) great fear is that Israel will succeed in toppling the "progressive" regimes now in power in Egypt and Syria and will install anti-Soviet governments in their place.[55] *Pravda* is therefore concerned about the impact of the war, especially of Israeli strategic bombing, on the economies of the Arab combatants.[56] Even an Arab victory, if sufficiently costly, could result in popular demands for an end of state socialism, a return to laissez-faire policies and a closer alliance with the United States in order to obtain American aid. Even more frightning is the specter of fresh Israeli conquests, which would surely discredit the existing governments and might even lead to their replacement by Israeli military rule.[57]

Worst of all, in *Pravda's* eyes, is the possibility of a U.S.–Soviet confrontation if the fighting continues. More than the other papers, *Pravda* is impressed by the seriousness of the situation in the Middle East, aware, as it puts it, of the danger that the conflict might be broadened, and anxious to prevent this.[58]

Given these fears and objectives, what policy does *Pravda* advocate? We would expect it to support a cease-fire, if not from the outset, at least after the Israelis had broken through Syrian lines and inflicted serious damage on Syrian plants, port facilities, oil refineries and power stations. *Pravda* does give the fullest report of all the papers on Israeli military successes, first on the Syrian, then on the Egyptian front, as if to make the case that the Arabs are losing and should welcome a cease-fire, even a cease-fire in place.[59] And it does hint, fairly early in the war, that a cease-fire might be desirable.[60] But these are only hints, of the most indirect sort. *Pravda* avoids direct discussion of a cease-fire until the Egyptians have accepted it. Whatever pressure Brezhnev may have wished to put on the Arabs to halt the fighting,[61] he did not regard the Soviet media as an appropriate instrument for exerting it.

But if *Pravda* does not push for a cease-fire and, like the other newspapers, repeatedly affirms Soviet support for the Arab cause, it does reveal very great eagerness to limit Soviet involvement in the war. Whatever might reduce or eliminate the need for Soviet participation this paper enthusiastically endorses. It calls for international aid (usually of an unspecified sort) to Egypt and Syria,[62] welcomes broader Arab participation in the war[63] and supports the use of oil as a weapon in the struggle.[64]

Given the apparent discomfort with the volatile situation in the Middle East expressed by this paper, why does it and those for whom it speaks support Soviet involvement in the area? *Pravda* does not have either a clearly articulated or a distinctive position on this question. Like all the other papers, it indicates a strong, but not explicit Soviet strategic interest in "this region, so close to our borders."[65] There is a suggestion that *Pravda* is also interested in the Middle East because many of the states in the area have advanced relatively far along the path to socialism, are eager for close economic ties to the USSR and the socialist bloc, and are thus likely to be reliable allies of the Soviet Union.[66] *Pravda* intimates, too, that it wants to deny the region's resources to the West.[67] And underlying and informing *Pravda*'s discussion of the Middle East is a fear and hatred of Zionism, suggesting a powerful unconscious sense on the part of Brezhnev and his supporters of a common cause with the Arab states.[68]

Pravda's reluctance to deal explicitly with the rationale for Soviet involvement in the Middle East contrasts sharply with its repeated defense and explanation of the Soviet search for detente. One is led to suspect that Brezhnev himself may be

20

ambivalent as to the desirability of a major Soviet involvement there, particularly on the scale of that which existed up to the outbreak of the 1973 war.

Pravda's treatment of future Soviet policy toward the area suggests such doubts. On many, many occasions it stresses the need for and Soviet interest in achieving a peaceful settlement of the Arab-Israeli conflict and avoiding further "military flare-ups." It does so far more often than the other papers, suggesting that there is considerable disagreement within the Soviet political elite on the desirability of this objective.[69]

Pravda's eagerness for peace in the Middle East seems to flow first of all from a combination of fear of a U.S.–Soviet confrontation and commitment to detente (which can help prevent one). So long as the Middle East remains a hotbed of war, *Pravda* avers, the relaxation of international tensions cannot proceed, but will be "interrupted by more and fresh outbreaks of conflict."[70] "... the settlement of the Middle East crisis would undoubtedly promote the improvement of the entire international situation."[71] Moreover, the conflict must not be resolved by further resort to arms. It must be setteled by "political," i.e., diplomatic, and not military means. *Pravda* is quite explicit about this: there must be no further "military flare-ups."[72] The "realistic" way to achieve peace is to reach a political settlement.[73]

But *Pravda* has a second reason for advocating a peace settlement, beyond its concern for the impact of the conflict on U.S.–Soviet relations. The Party newspaper, following Brezhnev, envisions a role for the USSR in implementing and guaranteeing a settlement.[74] This is very much *Pravda*'s cause. While the other newspapers rarely, if ever, discuss this idea, *Pravda* refers to it quite often.[75] It apparently reflects the hopes of Brezhnev and his supporters to achieve an arrangement which will offer the USSR the benefits of involvement without the present costs. A settlement guaranteed by the USSR will eliminate the threat of war and at the same time both legitimize and secure some kind of Soviet presence in the Middle East.

21

The United States could not later object to it nor the Arabs terminate it.

For what kind of settlement does *Pravda* think the USSR should strive? As usual, it is vague but suggestive. It makes many allusions to resolutions and decisions of the United Nations as a basis for a settlement,[76] but does not indicate which it has in mind. If these were *Pravda*'s only comments on the subject, one could not rule out the possibility that the paper and its patrons support radical Arab demands for a revision in their favor of Israel's 1967 borders, perhaps even a return to the 1947 partition plan. But *Pravda* intimates that it supports "the right of the State of Israel to sovereign existence."[77] More than that, it emphasizes the "legitimate" and "inalienable" rights and interests of "*all* states and peoples in the region"[78] and of providing "secure borders" and "security" to *all* countries in the Middle East.[79] This is extremely conciliatory language for the press of a country friendly to the Arabs. It suggests a very great eagerness for compromise with the United States and Israel.

Pravda's line on the question of the territory from which Israel should be expected to withdraw is similarly more moderate than that of the other papers, although the contrast is not as clear cut as in the case of *Pravda*'s concern for bringing peace to the Middle East. All the Soviet newspapers use a variety of formulations on the question of Israeli withdrawal. On some occasions they insist on "*complete* withdrawal" from "*all* occupied territories," a very broad demand, which could be interpreted to mean that Israel must withdraw from territory acquired in 1948 as well as 1967. At other times most of the major newspapers omit the word "complete" and call for simply "withdrawal" from "*all* occupied territories," thus at least leaving open the possibility that a less than complete withdrawal is acceptable. And occasionally one finds the demand for "complete withdrawal" or "withdrawal" from "occupied *Arab* territories," a more qualified formulation which allows for negotiation of the question which territories are Arab. The formula which *Pravda* uses most often is potentially the most

22

generous to Israel: it omits the words "complete" and "all," intimating that some new territory may be kept.[80]

Of course *Pravda*, like Brezhnev in his public speeches, does not say what the Soviet Union should or will do to induce or compel the Arabs to compromise on the issue of territory. But it is none the less significant that *Pravda* distinguishes itself from the other papers by its apparent willingness to consider at least small adjustments of Israel's 1967 borders so as to render them more secure.

A paradox arises at this point, however. If *Pravda* is so anxious for a peace settlement, why does it also give the Palestinians more enthusiastic backing than any other Soviet newspaper? Why does it support not merely the fulfillment of their "rights" or "legitimate rights,"[81] a deliberately ambiguous phrase employed by many governments anxious for peace in the Middle East, but also the "national rights" of the Arab people of Palestine?[82] Of course, this formulation is also ambiguous. But if *Pravda* wanted to be as cautious and circumspect as possible in its support of Palestinian demands, it surely would confine itself to "legitimate" rights and not characterize them. It would thus better avoid the appearance of support for Palestinian political aspirations and territorial claims. Why, moreover, does *Pravda*, alone of all the major Soviet newspapers, print a statement asserting that the "Palestinian resistance movement" represents the Arab people of Palestine?[83]

It might have been realistic for *Pravda* to assume that in the context of a real peace agreement, Israel might conceivably be persuaded to withdraw her troops from "occupied Arab territories," as defined in a prior process of negotiation — perhaps even "completely" and from "all" of them. But a Soviet demand that Israel must make political or territorial concessions to the Palestinians could only make the achievement of a peace settlement much more difficult, if not impossible. This is even more true of a Soviet demand that Israel accept Palestinian terrorists' claims to speak for all Palestinians. (It is important to remember that this antedates by almost a year United Nations recognition of the PLO. *Pravda* is, therefore, not merely bowing to the pressure of world or third world opinion.)

Is *Pravda*'s position internally inconsistent? Does it reflect conflicting sentiments within the Party apparatus, with some groups maintaining that peace is of overwhelming importance to the USSR and others that, in the light of Chinese competition in the third world, the USSR cannot afford to ignore a bona fide national liberation movement? Is Brezhnev himself ambivalent on this score?

All these interpretations are possible and cannot be ruled out. However, it is likely that *Pravda*'s position, and that of its patron, are, in fact, quite consistent: Brezhnev and his supporters see that, improbable as it may be, Israeli recognition of the national rights of the Palestinians and of the influence which resistance leaders have among them is a necessary condition for a peace settlement. It may be more difficult to reach an agreement with these elements in the picture, but it is impossible to reach one without them. That *Pravda* thinks the Palestinians are a major force to be reckoned with is indicated by the fact that it devotes a great deal of attention to their role in the fighting. This extensive coverage gives the impression that even if the Arab leaders dared make a settlement with Israel which did not take into account Palestinian demands, the Palestinians would ultimately undermine it through acts of guerilla warfare.[84]

Assuming that *Pravda* does speak for Brezhnev and for others in the Party who share his views or think it prudent to support them, we would like to know whether the General Secretary's approach to the Middle East has found support or opposition from other members of the Soviet political elite. Are there other equally ardent proponents of detente, and if so, do they hold the same views on the Middle East? If there are some who do not give detente and avoidance of Soviet–American confrontation the priority Brezhnev does, how does this affect their ideas on what Soviet Middle Eastern policy should be? Are all as interested as Brezhnev seems to be in the Soviet Union's current allies and, indeed, in maintaining and strengthening a Soviet presence in the Middle East? What other differences are there among Soviet elite opinion groups with regard to this region and their country's involvement there?

2.

No individual or group seems to be as anxious for detente as Brezhnev and his supporters. No paper devotes to it the proportion of space which *Pravda* does; none defends it as ardently. But of all the major groups whose views can be ascertained through the Soviet press, that which takes the position closest to Brezhnev's on this issue consists of Kosygin and the other state and economic officials for whom *Izvestiya* speaks.[85] Apparently these individuals attach great importance to Western trade, technology and investment in the USSR. They may also feel that detente can promote Soviet economic progress by making possible a reduced rate of growth of defense expenditures.[86]

Izvestiya does not make as much of an effort as *Pravda* to relate detente to Soviet interests in the Middle East or the interests of the USSR's friends in the region. But like *Pravda*, it does indicate to both internal and external skeptics that Soviet and American aims there are compatible.[87] It likewise makes some attempt to dissociate the United States and Israel, to absolve America of responsibility for the conduct of her client.[88] And if anything, it tries even harder than *Pravda* to persuade doubtful Americans of the moderation of Soviet policy in the Middle East and the eagerness for peace on the part of the states the USSR supports there.[89]

Izvestiya is, like *Pravda*, impressed by the seriousness of the situation in the Middle East, by the danger inherent in a clash between the clients of the two superpowers and the damage the war could do to the carefully constructed edifice of detente.[90]

Like *Pravda*, it welcomes measures which would bring the war to a speedy end. But there are interesting differences in the treatment of the subject by the two papers. *Izvestiya* pays less attention to political and military means and more to economic measures which could be used for this purpose. It evinces less interest than *Pravda* in promoting Arab unity and obtaining broader Arab participation in the war, and more interest in economic sanctions which might be taken against Israel.[91] *Izvestiya* also gives much more emphasis than *Pravda* to the economic vulnerability of the West and the benefits the Arabs could gain from exploiting it.[92] Probably the editors of *Izvestiya* are more elert to the degree of dependence of Israel on foreign trade and the West on Middle Eastern oil than are the ideologues or "generalists" who shape *Pravda*'s editorial policy.

Another very important difference between the reactions of *Pravda* and *Izvestiya* to the outbreak of hostilities is in the degree of alarm with which this event is initially greeted. During the first ten days of the war, one detects less of a sense in *Izvestiya* than in *Pravda* that there is an urgent need to stop the fighting and prevent further Israeli military successes.[93] What accounts for this difference?

In the first place, *Izvestiya* does not seem equally concerned about the fate of the regimes the USSR supports in the Middle East. It is understandable that state officials and economic administrators would not be particularly pleased by the performance of the Syrian and Egyptian governments or impressed by their allegedly "progressive" character. From the point of view of this group, if the current leadership in each of the "frontline" countries were replaced by one less radical and more devoted to economic development (and repayment of foreign debts), this might well be in the interest of the USSR. Quite possibly this is the reason that Kosygin and elites with a managerial background like his do not seem as perturbed as Brezhnev and other Party apparatchiki by the prospect that Israeli bombing and battlefield successes might discredit the governments in power.

Secondly, the economic officials for whom *Izvestiya* speaks seem to be more confident about the durability of detente. They are convinced that the emerging Soviet–American relationship has much to offer a variety of important interests in the United States. *Izvestiya* speaks of a powerful coalition of "responsible politicians" and "respectable businessmen," backed by the American public at large, which is pushing the American government toward the policy of detente.[94] The implication is that these powerful forces have too much to gain from this policy to allow their government to let it lapse.

The more relaxed attitude toward the fighting which *Izvestiya* at first seems to adopt may also reflect a stronger conviction on Kosygin's part than on Brezhnev's that the new relationship between the world's two most powerful states will itself prevent an escalation of the conflict and a confrontation between them. *Izvestiya*, in fact, seems to scoff at *Pravda*'s more cautious stance. Great positive changes have already occurred in international life, *Izvestiya* declares. Detente, constructive dialogue and cooperation are already a reality, already "actually exist and are yielding tangible results."[95] Why, then, is *Pravda* so fearful of a superpower collision? Kosygin, with personal memories of crisis-management by hot line in the previous Middle East war, may have initially felt more certain than Brezhnev that a U.S.–Soviet agreement could be reached to limit escalation.[96]

However, the most important reason why *Izvestiya* initially gives the impression that it is less anxious to end the fighting is that this newspaper is delighted by the impact of the war on the Western alliance. *Izvestiya* is not the only Soviet paper to report the conflict among the Western allies on the question of support for Israel.[97] But what the other papers deem worthy of occasional mention becomes in *Izvestiya* a central theme. *Izvestiya* follows the debate on this question in the British Parliament and happily announces that the House of Commons has approved an embargo on aid to the combatants.[98] The government newspaper also describes a deep split between the United States on the one hand and Western Europe and Japan

27

on the other over the issue of the U.S. resupply effort.[99] From the point of view of Kosygin and his supporters, strains in the Western alliance may be as beneficial to the USSR as detente (perhaps more so), and it is worth taking some risks to allow such strains to deepen and develop.

There is a limit to how much risk Kosygin is willing to take, however. On the night of October 15, Israeli forces cross the Suez Canal. They are still crossing when, on October 16, Kosygin leaves for Cairo. On October 17 *Izvestiya* begins reporting substantial Israeli successes.[100] The next day it notes the presence of U.S. helicopters and aircraft carriers in the Mediterranean and speculates that another aircraft carrier will soon be attached to America's "chief strike forces" in that ocean.[101] "An awareness of the unacceptability and even inadmissibility of solving international contradictions and disputes by military means is penetrating increasingly deeply into political circles and the broad popular masses in many countries," *Izvestiya* now writes in an article entitled "Peace Is Our Banner."[102] In the eyes of *Izvestiya* and its Politburo patron, there is now no question but the time has come to call for a cease-fire.[103]

It is at this time (after the canal crossing) that *Izvestiya* begins to emphasize that the Arabs have at their disposal effective alternatives to war. It points out the alarm generated in the West by recent Arab moves to control the supply of oil, reduce the amount available for sale and increase the prices at which it will be offered.[104] It warns of the economic disaster Israel's supporters will bring on themselves if they fail to "draw the appropriate conclusions" from these new departures in Arab oil policy. It predicts increasing support in the United States for the view that America must "treat the demands of Arab countries more attentively and the position of Israel more critically than up till now."[105] It even cites the Western press to demonstrate the potency of the new weapon in the Arab–Israeli conflict:

Whatever the pressure exerted by the Jewish community in America, the masses of the American people and of course the American government cannot fail to understand that it is in the interests of the American national economy to promote a settlement of the [Middle] East crisis..."[106]

There are measures short of war which may be equally or more effective, *Izvestiya* seems to be saying.

However, *Izvestiya*'s interest in the oil weapon does not stem (like *Pravda*'s) primarily from its importance as a substitute for war. What most impresses *Izvestiya* is the potential impact of the new Arab oil policy on Western political and military unity. It seems quite clear that this policy is the chief cause of Western division over support for Israel, and that it can continue to have a divisive effect on the Western alliance even if the Arab–Israeli dispute is resolved. *Izvestiya*, in fact, now initiates something of a campaign to encourage the Arabs to keep putting economic pressure on the West even after the fighting has stopped. Arab actions have already succeeded in bringing to the surface fundamental conflicts of interest among the capitalist states, *Izvestiya* points out. Continued pressure will surely deepen them:

For all the instinctive striving of [the] imperialist powers for a "united policy" with respect to [the] Arab countries, the interlacing of their interests turns out to be so complex, multiplaned and contradictory, that informed Western observers consider the probability of such united action as "insignificantly slight."[107]

What particularly pleases *Izvestiya* is the likelihood that the United States will suffer most in the new situation. It cites predictions in the Western press of "a mad, mad fight for Arab oil" and quotes *Newsweek* to the effect that within the Western alliance

"each side is convinced that the others will be ready to snatch what they can on the principle that 'charity begins at home' ... And the Japanese and the West Europeans will have the advantage over the United States in this competition: they are not tied like the United States by special relations with Israel ..."[108]

29

Such a three-cornered struggle will have "considerably more serious consequences than merely economic ones," *Izvestiya* gloats. Again invoking the authority of *Newsweek*, it goes on to forecast profound changes which will take place in the international system if the Arabs only keep up the good work:

"If competition for petroleum begins, then it will be virtually impossible to keep it from turning into a political and diplomatic war. In that case the whole postwar system of U.S. alliances with West Europe and Japan could be shattered ..."

The "problem of Arab petroleum" is certainly acquiring a new scale, *Izvestiya* concludes triumphantly.[109]

Given its interest in detente, it is surprising that *Izvestiya* manifests such obvious pleasure in the West's (and especially America's) new troubles. One can only surmise that with its confidence in the durability of detente, *Izvestiya* does not think it has much to lose. Why worry if a few American politicians will be irritated? A shortage of oil could only make Western business and Western governments more eager to invest in the development of Soviet energy resources. And if the Western economy is hurt by higher oil prices, profits will decline and (according to Leninist logic) the search for foreign markets and investment opportunities will be intensified. Economic necessity will keep detente alive.

Izvestiya's concern for and awareness of the economic aspects of international relations may provide us with a clue as to what this newspaper and the managerial interests it represents think the USSR should work for in the Middle East. One cannot detect in this newspaper the eagerness one found in *Pravda* to weaken international Zionism. There is almost no mention of the subject during the period of the war. An objective in which *Izvestiya* does display interest is the reopening of the Suez Canal. When the Middle East News Agency reports that the Suez Canal Authority has begun preparations for clearing the canal and expects to reopen it to navigation within six months, most of the Soviet press ignores this announcement. *Izvestiya* gives it a prominent place in its report on the "latest news" from the Middle East.[110] (How the opening of the canal will benefit the USSR economically *Izvestiya* does not say. One can only imagine that it anticipates increased Soviet trade with Southeast and Southcentral Asia, Subsaharan Africa and Russia's friends on the Persian Gulf. It may also calculate that if Egypt receives canal revenues, it will be less in need of Soviet aid and perhaps even capable of repaying its debts to the USSR.)

If opening the canal is a matter of great importance to *Izvestiya*, this would explain why it echoes, albeit with less avidity, *Pravda*'s interest in a Middle East peace settlement.[111] It would also account for *Izvestiya*'s similarly conciliatory stance on the question of Israel's borders. (Like *Pravda*, it emphasizes the necessity of assuring "secure borders" to "all states in the region" and "security" to "all countries and peoples" in the Middle East.[112]) Only if one satisfies the legitimate concerns of all the parties can one resolve the dispute, *Izvestiya* seems to be arguing,[113] and only a resolution of the dispute will insure peace and sustained operation of the canal.

With regard to the character of the peace settlement which the USSR should attempt to achieve, *Izvestiya*'s position differs from *Pravda*'s in one important respect. Like *Pravda, Izvestiya* stresses the need to implement the "legitimate rights of the Arab people of Palestine."[114] But it is vaguer on what those rights are. It does not express support for Palestinian "national" rights or for the leadership claims of the Palestinian resistance movement. By and large, *Izvestiya* pays less attention to the Palestinians, both as parties to the conflict and as participants in war. One can infer that Kosygin and other state officials are less impressed by their political and military achievements, less convinced that the USSR must support their demands if it wants to prevent another war in the Middle East. Certainly they are less concerned that the USSR will lose face if it fails to champion their cause.

In general one senses that Kosygin and *Izvestiya*, like

Brezhnev and *Pravda,* are concerned about the Middle East less for its own sake or the sake of what the USSR might accomplish there than for the bearing of events in the region on Soviet interests elsewhere in the world. But for *Izvestiya* the connection is less problematic, less troublesome. It believes Soviet global interests have been less endangered than furthered by recent developments in the Middle East. While a new war in the area is to be avoided, the USSR has definitely gained from this outbreak of hostilities.

3.

Krasnaya Zvezda seems to draw the same conclusion, but it arrives at it by an entirely different route. Its position therefore sharply contrasts with that taken by both *Pravda* and *Izvestiya* on most issues connected with the Middle East.

To begin with, *Krasnaya Zvezda* takes a stand on detente which is quite dissimilar to that of *Pravda* and *Izvestiya.* This is not to say that it is opposed to detente. It does not criticize it and occasionally even indicates support for it.[115] But it does not go out of its way to praise or defend it and does not attach great importance to it. Rather than dwelling on the benefits of detente, the organ of the Defense Ministry emphasizes that there are essential preconditions for it: high levels of Soviet strength and global activism.[116] Moreover, *Krasnaya Zvezda* intimates that the future of detente is uncertain because America's commitment to it is questionable.[117] Most important for Soviet policy in the Middle East, this newspaper does not (like *Pravda* and to a lesser degree *Izvestiya*) evaluate major world events in terms of their ability to promote or jeopardize detente.

Accordingly, we do not find *Krasnaya Zvezda* evincing anxiety about the effect of the war on detente.[118] In general, this newspaper tends to ignore the dangers in the situation created by the war and shows little interest in halting it. On the contrary, it supports Egypt's avowal of determination to "do everything in its power" to stop Israeli aggression.[119] Moreover, when even the comparatively sanguine *Izvestiya* has concluded that hostilities must be ended, *Krasnaya Zvezda* is still encouraging the Egyptian army to go on fighting, wishing it "further successes in the struggle against imperialist aggression."[120]

Insofar as *Krasnaya Zvezda* is disturbed by the outbreak of hostilities, its fears are quite different from those of *Pravda* and *Izvestiya*. It is first of all worried that the Arabs might fight badly, thereby discrediting Soviet arms and training in the eyes of the Arabs and the world. It eagerly reports Arab military successes and is generally silent about their setbacks, thus trying to create the impression that the Soviets' allies are invincible. It attempts to reinforce this impression with glowing accounts of the battlefield performance of the Arab armies — accounts which stress the quality of the equipment and training the soldiers have received.[121]

This emphasis on the Soviet contribution to the Arab war effort in turn reflects *Krasnaya Zvezda*'s second major concern. It is afraid that the USSR might appear unable or unwilling to give its friends the aid they need in time of crisis. It is highly sensitive to possible (or actual) Arab criticism of the USSR for lack of support and angrily denounces unspecified "attempts to create doubts about Soviet-Arab friendship."[122] The Soviet Union, it insists, is "faithful to its principled policy of support for the peoples striving for freedom and independence" and "acts consistently as the Arab states' reliable friend."[123]

But it is not only *Arab* reactions to Soviet behavior which worry the organ of the Defense Ministry. It is also concerned about the conclusions which will be drawn in the West and in Eastern Europe with regard to Soviet military capabilities and political will. How will Kremlin-watchers in Washington and Bonn, and more importantly in Warsaw and Budapest, evaluate Soviet conduct during the war? Will they interpret Soviet restraint as a sign of weakness, or inability or unwillingness to support its allies? *Krasnaya Zvezda* carefully scrutinizes the treatment in the bourgeois and socialist press of the Soviet role in the war.[124] In Eastern Europe, it somewhat nervously reassures its readers, the Soviet government statement on the war is viewed as "proof of the faithfulness of the USSR to its international obligation to support the friendly Arab countries."[125]

Given that *Krasnaya Zvezda* appears to be less concerned about the dangers of escalation than about the possible consequences of Soviet restraint, we would expect this newspaper to support a more direct Soviet role in the fighting when it becomes clear that the Arabs are in difficulty and Soviet interests jeopardized. There is some indication, albeit highly veiled, that *Krasnaya Zvezda* does advocate such a course. After the Israeli air force has begun to cause grave damage to Syrian cities (carrying out a series of air raids which destroy the Soviet cultural center in Damascus, inflict casualties on Soviet personnel in the building, and sink a Soviet merchant ship in the Syrian port of Tartus), *Krasnaya Zvezda* explodes with rage: "The aggressor's effrontery knows no bounds!" This time, it declares Israel has "gone too far." It had better interpret the Soviet government statement on the war as a "serious warning," which, if not heeded, will "entail serious consequences for Israel itself."[126]

It is not clear what action *Krasnaya Zvezda* is advocating. It seems to be using the bombing incident to argue that Israel cannot be allowed to embarrass the USSR in this fashion. In attacking Soviet citizens and Soviet property it has taken a step which demands, or at least justifies, something more than a verbal response from the Soviet Union. If such acts are repeated, *Krasnaya Zvezda* seems to be saying, the USSR will take measures to stop them.

The more desperate the Arabs' situation grows, and hence the more awkward Russia's position, the more belligerent the newspaper's language becomes. After Israel's successful canal crossing, *Krasnaya Zvezda* columnist Leontyev declares in an article entitled "Those Who Have Lost Their Heads,"

The sadists from Tel Aviv ... are following in the footsteps of the Hitlerites ... But it would do them no harm to remember how Hitler ended in his time ... The lessons of history cannot be ignored ...[127]

What are those lessons? Leontyev quotes a TASS dispatch which was issued earlier in the war, warning that "agression cannot go unpunished" and "the aggressor must bear strict responsibility for his acts."[128]

The key question, of course, is who will inflict this punishment and insure that the "aggressor" is held responsible? Leontyev continues to quote the TASS dispatch, to the effect that "'the USSR cannot remain indifferent to the criminal acts of the Israeli military.'"[129] This seems to suggest that it is not merely the Arabs, but the *Soviet Union* which is affected by the course of the war and must act to protect its interests. *Krasnaya Zvezda*'s resurrection of an earlier Soviet warning to Israel, its repetition of it under new, more critical circumstances, and its simultaneous identification of the Israelis with the bitterly hated invaders of Russia may be part of an effort by this newspaper to rouse support for greater Soviet involvement in the war.

It is hard to imagine that Grechko and the military leaders for whom *Krasnaya Zvezda* speaks are any more prepared than Brezhnev, Kosygin and their supporters to contemplate a U.S.–Soviet military confrontation. Nor, with their skepticism regarding America's attachment to detente, could they assume (as Kosygin and *Izvestiya* seem to) that the new Soviet–American relationship will prevent a confrontation. Perhaps one should infer that certain groups in the military are prepared to take more risks in support of the USSR's Middle Eastern clients because they assume that a post-Vietnam America will not substantially escalate its involvement in the fighting.

But this only raises another question. What, in the eyes of *Krasnaya Zvezda* and the military men for whom it speaks, is at stake in the Middle East? Why should the Soviet Union take major risks there? This is not the kind of question to which one is likely to find a direct answer in the Soviet press. As we have seen, *Pravda* and *Izvestiya* do not offer one. There is no reason to expect *Krasnaya Zvezda* would be more forthcoming and indeed, it is not. However, it does provide some hints, from which one can draw tentative conclusions as to its position.

Along with *Izvestiya*, *Krasnaya Zvezda* evinces more interest than the other major Soviet papers in the Suez Canal and the prospects for reopening it.[130] Probably there is an influential group in the military which desires to guarantee Soviet ability to use the canal. This is important because it would enable the Soviet Black Sea fleet to reach the Indian Ocean quickly and thus play both a symbolic, and if necessary, a combat role in southern Asia. Moreover, in October, 1973, the USSR was in the process of developing what would become a substantial military presence on both coasts of Africa.[131] Defense Minister Grechko had been a strong advocate of this project. Thus some segments of the military must have been eager to have the canal open to facilitate access to these areas as well.[132]

Interest in the canal, combined with a desire for naval and air facilities in the Arab states involved in the conflict,[133] could help explain the eagerness of certain military groups for a strong Soviet presence in the Middle East. This, in turn, would account for the willingness manifested by *Krasnaya Zvezda* to provide the Arab combatants with the aid they desire, even if it means escalating the Soviet role in the war.

Interest in using the canal would certainly not indicate that the USSR should favor indefinite prolongation of the Arab–Israeli conflict and the periodic flare-ups of violence which it generates. On the contrary, one might argue that only with a peace settlement could the availability of the canal be assured. Thus one might expect that even within the military there would be substantial support for a settlement. However, if this is the case, there is no sign of it in *Krasnaya Zvezda*. Indeed, it is on the question of the desirability of a peace settlement that this newspaper differs most sharply from *Pravda*, and to a lesser degree *Izvestiya*. Whereas Soviet interest in a "lasting peace in the Middle East" is a constant refrain in the latter two newspapers, it is scarcely mentioned in the military organ.[134] While *Pravda* often asserts the necessity of a political solution to the conflict, *Krasnaya Zvezda* almost never does.[135] When *Pravda* and *Izvestiya* stress the Arab states' desire for a political settlement,[136] *Krasnaya Zvezda* maintains an eloquent silence. And it is similarly silent when *Pravda* and *Izvestiya* dwell on the dangers inherent in the absence of a settlement.[137]

One is led to conclude that there are groups within the military which were content with the status quo ante bellum, who prefer a situation of no war, no peace to one of peace. Such an attitude is consistent with the image of American timidity which seems to be held by those who determine *Krasnaya Zvezda*'s editorial policy. If the United States will go to great lengths to avoid a new outbreak of fighting, then there is little to fear in the absence of a settlement. It is also consistent with military aspirations to use the canal. With the Egyptian army on both banks, there is nothing to prevent its being reopened, even in the absence of peace.

Nonetheless, surely Grechko and the other custodians of Soviet military interests see some danger in the perpetuation of the conflict and superpower involvement in it. Surely the prospect for continued Soviet use of the canal would be brighter with peace than without it. Why, then, does *Krasnaya Zvezda* display no interest in a political solution? Or, to put it differently, why is it unwilling to endorse the "Brezhnev plan," a peace settlement in which the USSR is one of the guarantors?[138]

Most probably the military men for whom *Krasnaya Zvezda* speaks do not see this as a realistic basis for perpetuating or expanding Soviet influence in the Arab world. Politicians and administrators may envision third world states drawn to the USSR by ideological affinity or economic interest. Generals are more likely to point to their eagerness for Soviet arms. And in the case of the Arabs this eagerness will surely be greater in the absence of a peace settlement. *Krasnaya Zvezda* outlines Israel's arms expenditures in the six years after the June War and on the basis of these figures projects the outlay of an even larger sum, as high as $10 billion, in the next six years.[139] It is very likely that the Arab states will want to match, if not exceed this figure. However, this calculation was made on the assumption that Israelis would accept the increasing militarization of their society.[140] Would they do so if a peace agreement were reached? If not, if they insisted on a reduction of the military budget, might there not be similar pressure on the Arab leaders to redirect their societies' resources? And if they did so, would there still be a role for the USSR in the new environment? *Krasnaya Zvezda* does not spell out this argument, but considerations of this sort probably underlie this newspaper's attitude toward a peace settlement.

There is another problem with the Brezhnev plan, from the point of view of the military newspaper. It is predicated on some kind of international agreement, with Soviet and American participation, which would provide guarantees to both sides in the conflict. Such an agreement would unquestionably have to include an affirmation of Israel's right to exist and to retain at least her 1967 borders. It would be unlikely that the United States would settle for less. *Pravda* and *Izvestiya* are prepared to accept both these conditions, and possibly go even further to accommodate the U.S. and Israel. But *Krasnaya Zvezda* is not. Unlike *Pravda* and *Izvestiya*, it avoids mentioning Security Council resolution 242, which calls for respect for the sovereignty of "every state in the region," and which demands Israeli withdrawl only from "territories occupied in the recent [i.e., 1967] conflict."[141] *Krasnaya Zvezda* also carefully avoids the formulae which *Pravda* and *Izvestiya* constantly employ: the necessity of recognizing the "legitimate rights and interests of *all* states and peoples of the region," and of assuring "security" to "*all* countries and peoples" and "secure borders" to all states in the Middle East.[142] Far from endorsing an Israeli need for secure borders, *Krasnaya Zvezda* portrays even Israel's 1967 borders as illegitimate.[143]

Krasnaya Zvezda does not say why it does not want to

recognize Israel and its 1967 borders. Perhaps the reason is simply that it wants to encourage Arab militancy. But there may be another reason, too. Although it has a stake in the perpetuation of the Arab-Israeli conflict, the Defense Ministry organ may actually look forward to the day when, with the elimination of or radical change in the character of the State of Israel, America's most reliable foothold in the Middle East will be removed.

If this is the aspiration of military circles for whom *Krasnaya Zvezda* speaks, we can understand why those same circles would find the Brezhnev plan unpalatable. It would place the USSR in a position of guaranteeing Israel's existence and hence an American presence in the Middle East. More than that, it might even serve as a pretext for the introduction of American troops into the area (if, as is likely, the U.S. would insist on being co-guarantor of the peace settlement). If one is concerned primarily with the expansion of Soviet political influence in the Middle East, one might very well favor a plan whereby the USSR, through pressure on the United States, procures an Israeli withdrawl to the 1967 lines, and then guarantees that the evacuated areas remain in Arab hands. Such a scenario would undoubtedly enhance Soviet political prestige in the Arab world. But if one is concerned primarily with countering American global power, in part through the acquisition and protection of military facilities in the Middle East and Africa, then one would be likely to oppose any plan which might increase American troop strength in the Middle East (even if only nominally) and stabilize an American presence there. This may account for the differences between *Pravda* and *Krasnaya Zvezda* and between Brezhnev and Grechko on the subject of peace in the Middle East and Soviet guarantees of a settlement. (*Izvestiya*'s position, generally supportive of a settlement and Soviet guarantees for it, but less ardent in defense of it, can be explained by lesser interest in the region and a lesser sense of the urgency to reach an agreement on the part of Kosygin and many Soviet managers and economic administrators.)

These inferences regarding the views of *Krasnaya Zvezda* and an influential segment of the military help to explain another striking difference between the discussion of the Middle East in the organ of the Defense Minisrty and that in *Pravda* and *Izvestiya*. As noted earlier, *Pravda* appears to be impressed by the impact of the "Palestinian movement" and its "liberation struggle" on the conflict in the region.[144] It repeatedly reminds its readers of the importance of recognizing "the rights"[145] of the "Arab people of Palestine."[146] *Izvestiya* also makes this point, although less often.[147] But *Krasnaya Zvezda* virtually never discusses the rights of the Palestinians or their identity as a movement or people. When it does mention them, it is in terms of their contribution to the war effort. Reports of sabotage operations and strikes on Israeli troop concentrations in the occupied areas and Israel proper, conducted by "Palestinian partisans" or "guerillas," are included in some of *Krasnaya Zvezda*'s accounts of the fighting.[148] But there is no discussion or defense of Palestinian political objectives.

One reason for these differences in the treatment of the Palestinians may lie in the differences in the roles which Party and state organs are called upon to play and the functions a military newspaper is expected to fulfill. Some portions of the Soviet media must assume or be assigned the responsibility of displaying the Soviet Union's revolutionary credentials. They must emphasize Soviet identification with and support for any political group which is widely recognized in the third world as an anti-imperialist or national liberation movement. *Pravda*, and to a lesser degree *Izvestiya*, as the authoritative voices of the Party and state, seem to have been assigned this role. Thus, however uninterested in or unsympathetic to the Palestinians their editors may be, they must express some support for the political ambitions of these people. *Krasnaya Zvezda* has no such obligation, and this in itself partly explains this newspaper's silence on Palestinian rights or peoplehood.

There are other reasons for these divergent approaches. It was argued above that *Pravda*'s insistence on recognition of

Palestinian rights stems not merely from that newspaper's role as Party spokesman, but from the view of its patron that this step is essential to bring peace to the Middle East. It follows that if *Krasnaya Zvezda* speaks for groups in the military which are not interested in peace, it would have less incentive to urge recognition of Palestinian rights. And if, as was argued, *Krasnaya Zvezda* is primarily interested in securing naval and air-landing facilities in strategic locations around the globe, this, too, would give it little ground for interest in Palestinian rights. Even if the Palestinians were able to acquire territory of their own, and this did not seem likely in October 1973, it would be too close to Israel to be of much military use to the USSR. Furthermore, if the Palestinians were to be granted a state of their own, it would be very likely to be demilitarized. The Palestinians would thus be of less military value than they were in the October War, in which they could take diversionary actions behind Israeli lines.[149] Finally, it was argued that what Grechko and like-minded military leaders prefer in the Middle East is not war, but something quite different, a situation of no war, no peace. To achieve such a state, the Soviets would have to see to it that the political leaders in the area were moderate, rationally calculating men over whom the USSR could exert leverage. As the Palestinian leaders hardly fit this description, *Krasnaya Zvezda* is uninterested in developing ties with them.

4

The opinions of the Russian nationalist newspaper *Sovetskaya Rossiya* on issues related to Soviet policy in the Middle East are often similar to those of *Krasnaya Zvezda* — in some cases so much so that one is led to suspect a working alliance between the groups represented by these two organs. However, on most issues *Sovetskaya Rossiya* tends to be somewhat less extreme than the military paper, and it often gives the impression that it is trying to build a bridge or facilitate a compromise between Brezhnev and Grechko.

Like *Krasnaya Zvezda, Sovetskaya Rossiya* is no crusader for detente and does not attempt to defend it against internal critics. But the Russian nationalists do seem to be more interested in it than the military leaders for whom *Krasnaya Zvezda* writes, more hopeful that it can bring some benefit to the USSR. For one thing, they are less skeptical of America's intentions. *Sovetskaya Rossiya* portrays the American President as highly enthusiastic about detente, especially about the scale and scope of U.S.–Soviet cooperation.[150] It seems to be a source of pride to *Sovetskaya Rossiya* that the President of the United States should consider the Russian people worthy of partnership with the Americans in political, economic and even technological spheres.

With this more positive evaluation of the benefits from and chances for attaining a detente with the U.S. comes a measure of nervousness, not present in *Krasnaya Zvezda*, about the effect of the war on American appriasal of Soviet commitment to detente. Like *Krasnaya Zvezda, Sovetskaya Rossiya* carries an article discussing the Soviets' initial response to the outbreak of hostilities, the Soviet government statement of October 7. Both papers attempt to portray this statement as evidence of a strong Soviet commitment to the Arab cause. But *Sovetskaya Rossiya* casts the statement in a different light. It concludes its discussion of this document with a comment probably aimed at uneasy American officials. They should not fail to note that "The statement of the Soviet government is viewed by many newspapers as a clear confirmation of the peaceful foreign policy of the USSR, its aspirationto strengthen the tendency toward reduction of international tensions."[151]

Apparently the Russian nationalists whose opinions are reflected in *Sovetskaya Rossiya* are concerned lest Soviet conduct during the war give the impression that the USSR is unwilling to abide by the principles of detente. But they are equally concerned that the friends of the USSR might conclude that the Soviets are prepared to sacrifice them to detente. *Sovetskaya Rossiya* is particularly embarrassed that the emigration of Jews from the USSR to Israel, widely assumed to be a concession to the United States, has been allowed to continue up to and after the outbreak of war. Predictably, this policy is bitterly condemned by the Arab world. *Sovetskaya Rossiya* relates this criticism, perhaps in an effort to persuade the Politburo to halt the exodus, at least for the duration of the war.[152]

Above all, *Sovetskaya Rossiya* (like *Krasnaya Zvezda*) seems to fear that a policy of restraint on the part of the USSR will cause Arab and other third world leaders to disparage the value of Soviet friendship. Aside from any policy consequences, remarks critical of the USSR are intrinsically humiliating and unpalatable to the patrons of this newspaper. Like the military newspaper, *Sovetskaya Rossiya* constantly reiterates that the USSR is a reliable ally and frequently quotes the Arab press to demonstrate that it is regarded as such by its friends. It also pays close attention to the reactions of the rest of the third world to Soviet policy during the war and often quotes statements of support for Soviet actions emanating from developing countries.[153]

This nervousness about third world reactions to a policy of excessive restraint gives the reader the impression that in the first days of the war a Russian nationalist faction sided with some military leaders in urging greater Soviet involvement — perhaps the airlift of weapons which ultimately materialized. After the airlift went into operation, on October 10, *Sovetskaya Rossiya* quotes the Syrian Ambassador to France as saying, "'We always thought and think that the USSR will conduct an honorable and noble policy...'"[154] Very probably this statement is the Syrian reaction to the commencement of the airlift. In quoting it the Russian Republic newspaper seems to be saying, "You see, had we held back, the Arabs would be branding us dishonorable and ignoble."[155]

There is, however, no indication that once the airlift was underway, *Sovetskaya Rossiya* continued to press for more direct Soviet involvement in the war, as *Krasnaya Zvezda* may have done. Rather, like *Pravda* and Brezhnev, it tried to encourage a broader Arab contribution to the conflict — probably as a substitute for Soviet participation.[156]

The similarity between Russian nationalist opinion and the views of influential military leaders emerges again with regard to the question of Soviet stakes and objectives in the Middle East. *Sovetskaya Rossiya* displays an interest similar to *Krasnaya Zvezda*'s in the reopening of the Suez Canal, perhaps for similar reasons. Like *Krasnaya Zvezda*, the Russian Republic organ evinces a comparatively strong interest in Africa, although Uganda, rather than Somalia, is the most frequent object of its attention.[157] Also like *Krasnaya Zvezda*, *Sovetskaya Rossiya* does not spell out the grounds for its interest in this distant area of the world. One can imagine that the opinion groups it represents welcome the expansion of Soviet military power and political influence on this continent for its own sake. To individuals who are anxious to increase the power the prestige of the USSR, Soviet ability to supplant the West in this former bastion of colonialism must be quite gratifying.

Sovetskaya Rossiya also wants to curb Western, particularly American, influence in the Middle East itself. (Again there is a parallel with *Krasnaya Zvezda*.) Whereas *Pravda*, in the interests of detente, plays down the tensions in Arab-American relations generated or brought to the surface by the war, *Sovetskaya Rossiya* eagerly reports them. An Arab League statement in the United Nations denouncing American support for Israel as a "hostile act in relation to the Arab countries" is descreetly omitted from *Pravda*'s account of the events of the day but quoted in *Sovetskaya Rossiya*.[158] In a summary of the major wartime speech by Syrian President Assad, the Russian Republic paper features his warning that "those who aid Israel in aggression" should "reflect on the fact that a hostile position toward the Arab nation will affect their numerous interests in Arab lands." This portion of the speech is ommitted in the *Pravda* version.[159]

If Russian nationalism is aligned with some portions of Soviet militarism in its aspiration to strengthen the position of the

USSR at the expense of the West in the Middle East and Africa, it also appears to have another objective which does not interest military circles. *Sovetskaya Rossiya* seems particularly concerned to diminish the power and prestige of the world Zionist movement. *Krasnaya Zvezda* generally ignores this phenomenon: to professional military men it is not of military significance. But *Sovetskaya Rossiya* seems to regard it as a genuine threat to the USSR. Of course this newspaper's attacks on Zionism are in part a form of propaganda, designed to win support for Soviet involvement in the Middle East from a Russian audience largely indifferent to or resentful of that involvement. Its diatribes may even be intended in part for Arab consumption. But they also convey anxiety on the part of the editors and the groups for whom they speak. The picture of the Zionist movement which emerges from the pages of this newspaper is one of a mighty political force of international dimensions: a highly disciplined movement which disposes of formidable economic and human resources, and which can mobilize both money and manpower with astonishing speed. It is portrayed as possessing tremendous political influence in the West, especially in Congress and with the American public. It operates in alliance with Western imperialism, and this threatens "progressive" states and movements everywhere. It is responsible for the present war and for Israel's alleged history of aggression against the Arabs.[160]

What, according to *Sovetskaya Rossiya*, should the USSR do about this menace? First and foremost, it must weld an anti-Zionist alliance which is as wide as possible. The Russian Republic paper is noticeably non-discriminatory in its choice of friends for the USSR. In contrast with *Pravda*'s (and Brezhnev's) clear preference for "progressive" states, the Russian nationalist organ lauds "friendly relations and close cooperation between the USSR and the *progressive and patriotic* forces in the Arab world."[161]

Should the USSR encourage its allies to come to a political agreement with Israel? Unlike *Krasnaya Zvezda* and some segments of the military, *Sovetskaya Rossiya* and Russian nationalist circles do seem to desire this. The Russian Republic newspaper portrays the Arabs as interested in a settlement[162] and prints favorable comments on Brezhnev's efforts to achieve one.[163] However, *Sovetskaya Rossiya* does not dwell on the dangers inherent in the absence of a settlement. Nor does it display the sort of ardor for one which emerges from the pages of *Pravda*. The editors seem to be ambivalent. They are uncomfortable with the kind of crisis situations which are periodically created by the conflict in the Middle East.[164] Moreover, they believe that "Zionist expansionism" is aided by the absence of a settlement, presumably because it provides Israel with a pretext for going to war.[165] Nor are they confident that the Arabs, even with Soviet weapons and training, are an adequate match for the Zionist-imperialist alliance.[166] Thus even if a political settlement will legitimize the existence of the Zionist state, even if it will strengthen America's position in the Middle East, they are willing to accept it. But they are more restrained in their support for it than the individuals who determine the editorial policies of *Pravda*.

5.

If *Sovetskaya Rossiya* represents a mid-point on a scale of increasing militancy, with *Pravda* at the bottom and *Krasnaya Zvezda* at the top, then we can think of *Komsomolskaya Pravda* as occupying a very high position, next to or just below that of the military newspaper. Officially the organ of the Soviet youth organization whose name it bears, *Komsomolskaya Pravda* generally expresses the views expounders of Marxism-Leninism and self-appointed defenders of the faith, who have long sought and often been granted control over education, culture and youth affairs.

Of all the elite opinion groups to whose views we have access, this one seems to welcome the war in the Middle East with the least ambivalence and fewest reservations. One detects a sense of relief that at last the "Arab liberation forces" are behaving in a manner worthy of their name, that at last they are taking action to end a humiliating, burdensome and dangerous occupation of their territory. *Komsomolskaya Pravda* depicts the Arabs as having endured a long series of defeats at the hands of the Israeli aggressor. The most recent of these, in 1967, is portrayed as in some respects the most serious. The seizure of the Sinai deprived Egypt of its most valuable economic resources: oil, iron ore and manganese, and most important, Suez Canal revenues. Syria lost relatively little territory, but what was taken was of great strategic significance. Israeli troops occupying positions only a few kilometers from the Syrian capital created a constant threat, hanging over it "like a Damocletian sword." Now at last the humiliation could be ended, the burden lifted and the danger removed. *Komsomolskaya Pravda* virtually exults over the "new character" the conflict in the Middle East assumed with the outbreak of war.[167]

It is not surprising that ideologically orthodox groups should derive the greatest pleasure from the war. From their point of view, there is little to lose and much to gain by it. *Komsomolskaya Pravda* is the least enthusiastic about detente of all the major Soviet newspapers. It mentions detente only when absolutely necessary,[168] almost never independently praises or defends it, and attaches to it no major significance. Indeed, the reader of this newspaper would never know that the search for ways to reduce international tensions and increase international cooperation had been defined by his country's highest leader as the Party's main task and most important goal in foreign relations. The reason for this is that while detente can be and has been justified in ideological terms, it has always been ideologically suspect. Professional expounders of ideology have always been enbarrassed by it, as well as uneasy with its impact on Soviet youth and on Soviet society in general. Unlike certain segments of the military, they are not comforted by the prospect that detente will lead to future strategic arms control agreements

DOMESTIC INFLUENCES ON SOVIET FOREIGN POLICY

favorable to the USSR. Thus one senses that as far as *Komsomolskaya Pravda* is concerned, if detente is impeded by the war in the Middle East, the Soviet Union will have no reason to grieve and will perhaps be better off.

If *Komsomolskaya Pravda* is unenthusiastic about detente, this is at least in part because it shares with *Krasnaya Zvezda* considerable skepticism concerning American commitment to it. In fact, it portrays the October War, and events in the Middle East generally, as evidence that the United States is pursuing an active and aggressive anti-Soviet policy. By encouraging Israeli aggression against the Arab countries, the U.S. is attempting to undermine the position of progressive Arab regimes, friendly to the USSR. Israel's actions have been taken to further the global interests of American imperialism, which has both "military-political" and economic ambitions in the Middle East. Soviet ideologues welcome the war as an opportunity to halt this process, to protect Soviet interests in the Middle East against American encroachment. The "aggressor" against whom the Arabs are defending themselves is merely an agent of another power, and the "resolute rebuff" of this power is very much in the USSR's interest.[169]

Consistent with its enthusiasm for the war and high hopes for its outcome, *Komsomolskaya Pravda* seems to advocate a Soviet air- and sealift to support the Arabs.[170] However, there is no clear evidence that this newspaper or the ideologues for whom it speaks desire more direct Soviet military involvement, even after the successful Israeli offensives in Syria and Egypt. The Komsomol paper supports "maximum material, medical and other aid to the Arab peoples [who are] victims of Israeli aggression,"[171] but it does not specify that this aid should be Soviet, much less that it should include Soviet troops or pilots. On the other hand, it makes very clear its enthusiasm for broader participation in the war on the part of other Arab states besides Egypt and Syria and welcomes the use of the oil weapon.[172]

If *Komsomolskaya Pravda* does not want the USSR to become

48

directly involved, this would seem to be less out of fear of the consequences of such a step than out of the conviction that it is unnecessary. As one might expect from professional expounders of Marxism, the ideologists for whom this newspaper speaks are sensitive to a variety of social forces and political conflicts and pressures which they claim working in the Arabs' favor. First there are those within Israel itself, where the Left is vigorously protesting the continuation of the war and the army command is too internally divided to wage war effectively.[173] Even more important is the pressure exerted on the governments of Western Europe by their own people. "The energetic actions of the progressive public" are forcing these governments to adopt a new position of neutralism vis-a-vis the Arab-Israeli conflict — to desist from aiding Israel. This new policy is already helping the Arabs by hindering the American operation to resupply Israel. Ultimately, the growing international solidarity with the Arab cause and against American-inspired Israeli expansionism will bring the Arabs victory. Imperialism will be forced to retreat in the Middle East, just as it was in Vietnam. (As good Marxists, the editors are noticeably vague with regard to the date when this is likely to happen.)[174]

If the Komsomol leaders and the ideologists who share their views are content to let the war in the Middle East take its course without direct Soviet intervention, if they are prepared to accept the cease-fire frantically sought by Brezhnev, it is not merely because they are confident that History is on the side of the USSR and its allies. It is also because they believe that from the point of view of both Soviet and Arab interests the war has been a very great success. One can now exploit and develop the gains already made. The tensions in the Western alliance sparked by the war will be of substantial benefit to the USSR. (*Komsomolskaya Pravda* does not give this theme the same attention and coverage it receives in *Izvestiya*, but it is clearly pleased by this development.[175])

Even more significant for the Komsomol newspaper is the impact it expects the war and the Soviet role in it are likely to have on Sino–Soviet competition in the Third World. The professional ideologists whose views are reflected in this paper are charged, among other things, with spreading Soviet ideology among Third World peoples and winning their allegiance to socialism and the Soviet Bloc. It is therefore of the utmost importance to them to be able to demonstrate Soviet interest in and assistance to these peoples, particularly to those who see themselves as engaged in a struggle against Western imperialism and "neo-colonialism." Thus of all the major newspapers, this one is the most sensitive to Chinese charges that the USSR has betrayed the national liberation movement in general and the Arab liberation struggle in particular, that it has sold out to the West and is collaborating with the imperialists to suppress revolutionary movements. Now *Komsomolskaya Pravda* can point with pride to events in the Middle East as evidence that the USSR and the socialist bloc (which in Soviet usage does not include China are "the main bulwark" of "the national liberation struggle of the peoples."[176] It can use various incidents in the war to demonstrate the depth of Soviet involvement and the extent of its influence in the "progressive" Arab states. When Israeli planes strike targets in Egypt, the Communist youth organ can recount Komsomol contributions to repair the damage caused by earlier raids. When the Soviet cultural center in Damascus is bombed, it is an occasion to describe the popularity of Soviet culture in Syria.[177]

Most important, *Komsomolskaya Pravda* can now boast of impressive Arab military accomplishments and the Soviet military equipment which made them possible. With the help of this equipment, this paper points out, Egyptian troops were able to cross the Suez Canal, overcome the Bar Lev Line (which Israeli strategists had touted as impossible), and destroy Israel's 190th Tank Brigade. Indeed, the commander of this brigade, captured by the Egyptians, admitted the superiority of Egyptian tanks on the field of battle.[178] Like *Krasnaya Zvezda, Komsomolskaya Pravda* cites western press reports commending the "first class Soviet arms" in the hands of the Arabs and attributing the success of Egyptian troops in the Sinai to them.[179] But more significant for this newspaper, speaking for groups anxious to win Third World approval of the USSR, are Arab press comments praising Soviet weapons. The Komsomol paper quotes at length from an Egyptian newspaper exulting that this war "is possibly the first time the Israeli air force with its modern U.S. fighters and bombers, fitted with sophisticated electronic equipment, has found itself in a position of helplessness." This, declares *Komsomolskaya Pravda,* citing the Egyptian source, is due to "missiles of Soviet manufacture [which] have changed the course of hostilities in the air."[180]

But if this newspaper is pleased by the credit the USSR has won in an important segment of the Third World, it is at least equally delighted by the devastating impact it believes the war has had on Israel. It is no exaggeration to say that the groups for which this newspaper speaks despise Israel and the ideology on which it was built. As *Komsomolskaya Pravda* portrays it, Israel is a state whose very existence is an affront to the conscience of mankind. The territory it occupies was seized from its rightful owners, the native Arab inhabitants of the land, whom the Israelis drove away by use of terror. This policy began even before the creation of the state, so that when the state was established there were already 900,000 Palestinian refugees. This brutal conduct was inspired by the ideology of Zionism, a militaristic creed which inculcates love of war and bloodshed and calls for the expansion of Israeli territory at the expense of Arab lands. Since the establishment of the state, Israelis have demonstrated their devotion to Zionist teachings by continuous aggression against their Arab neighbors. Israel's first act of foreign policy was the seizure of 7,000 square kilometers of land designated by the United Nations for Arab control. In subsequent years the Arabs were again and again robbed of territory, with the biggest "theft" occurring in 1967. The history of Israel is thus the "history of the crimes of Zionism."[181]

It is not obvious why, of all the major groups within the

Soviet political elite, the professional ideologues should harbor the most intense animus against Zionism and the society founded on it. Perhaps one reason for this is that this group takes ideas and ideologies more seriously than any other. It is thus likely to pay more attention and attach more political significance to Zionism as a set of ideas and guide to action. (For *Sovetskaya Rossiya*, by contrast, "Zionist" is simply a label attached to any one or any group which supports Israel. The Russian nationalist newspaper is uninterested in Zionism as a set of ideas or in the society dedicated to those ideas; it is exclusively concerned with the international influence the supporters of Israel can muster.)

For Soviet ideologues Zionism is an object of fascination and hatred because it is a rival, and a successful one, to Communism. Expounders of Marxism-Leninism are not known for their affection for competing creeds, especially those which have been aimed at the same or overlapping audiences — in this case the Jews in the Soviet bloc, as well as the Jewish proletariat in Europe and America before the Second World War. (A similar animus against Social Democracy and Social Democrats can also be detected in *Komsomolskaya Pravda*.)

Moreover, the professional defenders of the values and goals of Communism, the men charged with maintaining the ideological morale of Soviet society and winning the minds and hearts of the uncommitted abroad and the young at home, are the most likely to feel bitter personal resentment of Zionism. Some of them are sincere believers in the doctrine they teach — that is why they have chosen to teach it. The Soviet Jews who opt for Israel instead of the Soviet Union are rejecting and thus, in effect, challenging their fundamental convictions. But even for those who are not sincere believers, who do not stop to ask themselves what they believe, or who believe little of what they teach, there is considerable reason to resent Zionism. Every Jew who leaves or asks to leave makes their work more difficult. The appeal that Israel has for Soviet Jews is a sign that they have done their job poorly. (The appeal of the capitalist West is similarly troublesome, and the West and capitalist ideology are attacked with particular venom in *Komsomolskaya Pravda*.)

Zionism would be less offensive if it were less successful. The editors of *Komsomolskaya Pravda* regard it as eminently successful, and this helps explain why they are both infuriated and somewhat awed by it. There is something profoundly disturbing to them about a creed which can mobilize men to fight and to die for it: can Communism still do the same? Zionism's success has even enabled it to intimidate its opponents. *Komsomolskaya Pravda* speaks of "Zionist agitators" who were able to undermine the confidence of the Arab soldiers with the "myth of Israeli invincibility."[182] It has been no small task for Soviet political instructors to overcome the impact of this myth, and this newspaper expresses their frustration.

Their resentment of Zionism and the grip it has had, on the minds even of its enemies, helps explain the satisfation expressed by ideologists with the progress of the war, even when it has turned against the Arabs. Arab successes in the first days of the war were enough to dispel the myth that Zionism is invincible and the Zionist state undefeatable. "Whatever the future course of events in the Middle East," *Komsomolskaya Pravda* columnist Agaryshev writes on the day after Israel's successful canal crossing, "these myths have been shattered."[183]

This shattering of Zionist myths is intrinsically gratifying to Agaryshev: it is pleasant to be able to expose the falsehoods and demonstrate the failures of a hated rival creed. This will also make easier the job of Soviet advisers and political instructors working with Arab armies. But above all it will have far-reaching political results, profoundly important to the Arabs and eminently satisfying to the Soviet foes of Zionism. "The dissipation of myths," Agaryshev declares, is inevitably followed by political defeats. "Now even those who blindly believed the Zionists in everything are beginning to think twice." Lest anyone wonder to what he is alluding, Agaryshev spells it out quite clearly:

Those whom the Zionists persistently urge to abandon their native land and settle in Israel now know what these agitators are preparing for them. Those who finance Israel's military adventures see that their money is going into the dustbin of history.[184]

Even if the Arabs have not won on the battlefield, in other words, they have been sufficiently successful to show Jews everywhere what future Israel faces at the hands of Soviet-trained and -equipped Arab armies. Confronted with that image, rather than the illusory one of Israeli invincibility (Agaryshev predicts) Jews will cease to contribute their lives and substance to the Jewish state. Can Israel, so dependent on these contributions, then continue to exist? "The Israeli aggressors have already endured not only significant military and material losses, but also, what is especially important, *irreparable* political losses" Agaryshev concludes triumphantly.[185] For the ideologues for whom *Komsomolskaya Pravda* speaks, Israel's survival as a Zionist state is now, if not entirely precluded, at least an open question.

With this kind of attitude toward Israel and this evaluation of its political prospects, one would not expect the groups represented by *Komsomolskaya Pravda* to be interested in a political settlement in the Middle East — at least not in the short run. This, indeed, appears to be the case. *Komsomolskaya Pravda* is almost completely silent on the question of a political solution to the Arab–Israeli conflict, in striking contrast to *Pravda*'s (and Brezhnev's) eagerness for one.[186] This paper does indicate a desire for peace in the Middle East, but only under certain special conditions. Having argued that not merely the 1967, but even the 1948 borders of Israel are illegitimate, based on unjustifiable territorial aggrandizement, this newspaper condemns both Israel's refusal to allow the Palestinians the right to return to their native land and its policy of settling Jewish immigrants in the areas vacated by Arabs. Only after making this point does it declare its support for a "just and lasting peace in the Middle East."[187]

What kind of peace, then, would *Komsomolskaya Pravda*

consider just and lasting? One is led to believe that it would favor a peace agreement, but only on condition that Israel retreat to the areas allocated to it by the 1947 United Nations partition plan; that it allow the Palestinians to return and reclaim land, not merely on the West Bank and Gaza, but even within the territory of the new, reduced Israel. This newspaper may even be hinting that Israel should be prevented from bringing in more immigrants. Clearly, at any rate, the kind of Israel with which it wants the Arabs to make peace would be a very different entity, both geographically and demographically, from what it is today. Possibly the ideologues would settle for a less radical transformation. But it is likely that, in the aftermath of the October War, they see no need for such concessions. Like Grechko and the other military leaders for whom *Krasnaya Zvezda* writes, they do not seem to fear another prolonged period in which there is neither peace nor war and are not unduly alarmed by the possibility that another war might break out in the area. They are, therefore, in no hurry to compromise or ask their allies to do so.

One might well ask, if *Komsomolskaya Pravda*'s mentors are not afraid of instability in the Middle East, why do they support peace in any form, under any conditions? Are they not concerned (as some portions of the military appear to be) that peace will reduce the Soviets' ability to exert influence in the area? Possibly the answer to this question is that this segment of the Soviet political elite is more sanguine about the appeal of Soviet ideology. It has more confidence than the military in the ability of Soviet political ideas to win friends and influence people. Perhaps it believes that in conditions of peace revolutionary social forces, now distracted by the conflict with Israel, will begin to press harder for a socialist transformation of the Arab states. And when they do so, they will want Soviet advice, technical assistance and economic aid.[188]

There is a problem with this explanation of the position of *Komsomolskaya Pravda*: it seems to assume a kind of naivete, a lack of hard-headedness, which is not characteristic of Soviet politicians. The Soviets have been a good deal more successful at selling (and giving) arms than ideas and advice, especially on a sustained basis. This has been and is likely to be even more the case in the Middle East than in other parts of the Third World, where there is less antagonism between Communism and indigenous ideologies and beliefs.[189] One would expect professional ideologues to be aware of this. One would expect them to be aware, too, of the difficulty the USSR would have in competing with the West as a source of development assistance.

Undoubtedly Soviet ideologists are aware of these problems. But it is very likely that they have answers to them. The popularity of Communism is bound to increase with economic development, while the appeal of religious and nationalistic doctrines will diminish. The war against Israel has up to now prevented development and encouraged a preoccupation with Arab identity. When the problem of Israel has been satisfactorily resolved, resources will be released for development, social concerns will take precedence over national ones, and Communism will make more headway. The capitalist West will be none too eager to assist the development of socialist societies, and Soviet aid will be sought. Peace contains certain risks, but it also holds out attractive prospects.

Another clue to *Komsomolskaya Pravda*'s attitude toward peace in the Middle East may perhaps be found in this paper's frequent references to the Palestinians and its formulation of Palestinian rights. It pays more attention to the Palestinians than any other major paper.[190] As we have seen, it condemns their exclusion from the territories from which they have fled, thus going farther than any other major paper in support of Palestinian demands. At the same time, it prints several statements calling for implementation of the "national" rights of the Palestinians.[191] Perhaps all this is only an elaborate demonstration intended to show that the USSR is a friend of national liberation movements. But it is more likely that *Komsomolskaya Pravda* is genuinely eager for Palestinian friendship. Very probably it is hopeful with regard to the radicalism of the

Palestinian movement and its leadership. And it is gambling on continued American indifference to it, even after a peace settlement. Could the United States become a friend and patron of a movement so hostile to Israel and Zionism? Surely not. Thus if a Palestinian state were established to satisfy Palestinian nationalism, it would seek Soviet aid and protection. The USSR would have a foothold in the heart of the Middle East. Russia might even begin to play a role in Israel — an Israel with a substantial Arab returnee population — and eventually undermine America's position in the region. A vision of this sort probably underlies *Komsomolskaya Pravda's* stance on peace.

6.

The views of the trade union newspaper, *Trud*, on Soviet Middle Eastern policy are less fully articulated. Moreover, it is less clear what political group this paper represents. There is no question that it speaks for Alexander Shelepin, head of the Soviet trade union organization and a Politburo member until the spring of 1975. There is also little doubt that by October, 1973, Shelepin had amassed a sizeable band of followers in the trade union apparatus, and probably also in the Komsomol and the Security Police, each of which he had previously headed. But it is less clear how influential this group was and whether its members held similar and well-formulated opinions on foreign policy issues. We are probably safe in assuming that they did: police officers, youth leaders and trade union officials share a similar function in Soviet society, and this function tends to generate a common political outlook. Those who occupy responsible positions in these organizations are all in some way concerned with maintaining order and control. They are appointed because of their commitment to these objectives and their skill in implementing them. The requirements of their jobs, in turn, influence their attitudes. They tend to favor a high level of internal discipline, suppression of dissent and ideological deviation, and an emphasis on patriotism in education, culture and propaganda. For this reason they tend to be most comfortable with a foreign policy line which allows them to portray the West and capitalism as enemies of the USSR, bent on subverting Soviet society and Soviet values.

Shelepin himself is known for his hard-line, conservative positions on internal issues, but also for his pragmatism and adaptability. Prior to the October War, he had not spoken out on a wide range of external problems, although he had opposed the deterioration of Sino–Soviet relations and the pursuit of detente.[192] The youngest Politburo member, at one time one of the most powerful men in the country, Shelepin was once regarded as Brezhnev's most likely successor. After Autumn of 1965, his position was systematically weakened, but he was still considered an important rival and possible successor to the General Secretary until his removal from the Politburo. His personal ambition — his desire to develop positions distinctive from but not dangerously antithetical to Brezhnev's — may be the chief inspiration behind his policy pronouncements during the October War. The line taken by *Trud* probably reflects both Shelepin's private goals and the views of the control-oriented officials whom he promoted and whose support he enjoyed.

Trud is not merely unenthusiastic or reticent about detente. It mounts a concerted campaign to persuade its readers that, while a noble and enticing objective, it is an utterly unrealizable and unrealistic one. The problem with the policy of detente is that it assumes there has been and can be a major change in the character of international relations in general, and in U.S.–Soviet relations in particular. Some slight change there has been. "The world political climate has been growing warmer," *Trud* acknowledges.[193] However, there is a limit as to how far this process can go, and how significant the change is which has already occurred.[194] Neither should be overestimated. The reason for this is that the international system is still very much influenced by the power and ambitions of imperialist forces.

And as *Trud* puts it, "The positive changes in international relations by no means imply that imperialism has changed its essence."[195] Statesmen may wish for peace, may talk about the reduction of international tensions, but there are forces larger than they, thwarting their efforts:

...the threat to peace, flowing from the very nature of the aggressive actions of imperialism, continues to darken the international horizon.[196]

One cannot fail to consider that there are still powerful forces in the world which oppose a reduction of international tensions, oppose peaceful coexistence, do everything possible to blacken the international situation, interfere in the internal affairs of other countries and carry out ideological diversions.[197]

Trud does not say whether these powerful forces are embodied in any specific individuals, governments or institutions, and if so, which ones. The important thing is the extent and inevitability of their influence on international relations and their determination and ability to obstruct detente.

How is all this related to the war in the Middle East? Very directly. If for *Pravda* and Brezhnev the war demonstrates the usefulness and need for detente, for *Trud* and Shelepin it proves that detente is unattainable, that the forces which oppose it are more powerful than those which desire it. Imperialism is responsible for the war: it inspired and backed the Israeli provocations which caused it. Moreover, the war is, in fact, an effort on the part of imperialism to take revenge for detente. It is the clearest evidence one could want as to the unchanging nature and aims of imperialism.[198]

But what are the aims of imperialism, as manifested in this war? Why do they preclude detente? *Trud* does not spell this out, presumably believing the answer too obvious. But it does describe the policy and means imperialism employs: it uses violence and war to encroach on the independence and sovereignty of nations and prevent those peoples who are struggling for their independence and freedom from attaining it.[199] In the "recent Israeli aggression" the Arab peoples are the victims of this policy.[200] *Trud* builds its case carefully, until finally it arrives at this critical conclusion: "The recent aggravation of the situation in the Middle East is the result of … a policy which contradicts the entire contemporary development of international relations, and which is directed not only against the Arabs, but also against [world] peace …"[201] *Trud* announces what Brezhnev and Kissinger do not want to admit: this war is a violation of detente. It is not a temporary disturbance which can be smoothed over and isolated from the main course of Soviet–American relations. When the fighting has been halted in the Middle East, it will only erupt somewhere else. Whatever agreements are made about preventing conflict and preserving peace, imperialism is sure to violate them. It will never observe the principles of detente.

What are the implications of this conclusion for Soviet foreign policy? Clearly the USSR must not sacrifice any of its interests for the sake of detente. And it must not hesitate to oppose imperialist aggression whenever and wherever it occurs. It should "aid all peoples struggling for national liberation" and thereby "give a decisive rebuff to all intrigues of aggressive imperialist forces."[202]

Apparently *Trud*'s position is something like the following. The USSR should play an active role in the Third World, including the Middle East. It should offer both military and economic aid when this will enable it to win new allies or keep old ones — especially when it can reduce American influence and curtail American ambitions in a given region.[203] There is no reason to cooperate with the United States in "stabilizing" specific regions or international relations generally: the United States will not abide by such agreements.

One would very much like to know more specifically what course of action *Trud* and Shelepin are advocating, what they would have the USSR do in the Middle East. Unfortunately, *Trud* says little more on the subject. Possibly one can infer its position from its silence. Compared to the other major papers, even the military organ, it is conspicuously uninterested in peace in the Middle East. It does not talk about the importance of achieving a political solution there[204] and ignores the dangers inherent in the absence of one. It does not give the impression that the Arab states want to reach a settlement with Israel and omits comments by Arab speakers which might give that impression.[205] It gives no indication that it thinks Israel should be guaranteed "security" or "secure borders."[206] Even the "Brezhnev plan" for Soviet guarantees to all the parties to the dispute arouses no interest on the part of *Trud's* editors.

It is difficult to draw reliable inferences from silence, and even more difficult to explain the views one has inferred. It is possible that Shelepin and his followers oppose Brezhnev's efforts to achieve a negotiated settlement of the Israeli–Arab conflict and his scheme for Soviet guarantees of the settlement which is reached. It is also possible that Shelepin's silence reflects an unwillingness on his part to commit himself on an issue on which he does not have to. He has already made a strong stand on detente, made a bid, in effect, for the support of ideologues and military leaders in a future succession struggle. Why should he take a well-defined stand on the Middle East, too? By remaining silent he provokes no one and alientaes no potential supporters. Nor can one rule out the possibility that Shelepin actually has no clear position on the Middle East. Conceivably in October, 1973, he is not really sure what policy the USSR should pursue there, particularly whom it should support and what objectives it should endorse. Why not wait and see what impact the war will have on politics in the region: will the current leaders be strengthened or discredited; will Egypt be more cooperative or less; will the Palestinians gain or lose influence; and within the Palestinian movement will radicals or pragmatists gain the upper hand? Shelepin can only lose by being more explicit before these issues are clarified. Probably all these factors play a role in *Trud's* silence.

61

IV.

CONCLUSION

The nature of the source material requires that any and all conclusions be drawn with the greatest tentativeness. In addition to all the problems discussed at the outset, the analyst must keep in mind the very strong possibility that one or more of the newspapers studied presented only a partial picture of the opinions of the group or groups for which it speaks. Even if we assume that we have correctly identified these groups and that the positions taken by "their" newspapers accurately reflect their views, we may still be led astray if a few important elements in a group's position have been omitted or censored. Much of the reasoning and some of the conclusions reached in this analysis would have to be changed, for example, if it appeared that any one of the groups represented genuinely feared or favored a confrontation with China. If this is true of the military groups for whom *Krasnaya Zvezda* speaks, could they be as unenthusiastic about detente as they are portrayed here? We would have to make some amendments, too, if it turned out that questions have been raised about the Palestinians which have not been reported in the press. Are many ideologues skeptical of the socialist credentials of the Palestinian movement? If so, could they be as eager to champion the Palestinian cause as they are depicted in this study? This portrait of these elite opinion groups must be provisional, subject to change as more becomes known about their views.

What emerges from this study is that the starting point from which each of these elite opinion groups appears to formulate its Middle Eastern policy is its image of and attitude toward the West, most importantly, the United States, and its vision of the future of U.S.–Soviet relations. The images reflected in the press are of four general types: cooperative, competitive and antagonistic, and a hybrid of the first and third. There are thus four general tendencies of opinion with regard to the Middle East, each corresponding to one of these views of the United States and the U.S.–Soviet relationship.

1) adverse partner

This approach, taken by *Pravda*, and representative of the views of Brezhnev and his supporters in the Party apparatus, regards the United States as a potential partner in solving key international problems. The chief foreign policy objectives of those who take this view of the United States are the prevention of a U.S.–Soviet military confrontation, especially a nuclear confrontation, and a general reduction of international tensions. They believe in the possibility of "international relations of a new type," in which adversaries recognize certain common interests and act together to promote them. This, for them, is the meaning and purpose of detente.

Those who subscribe to this approach are impressed by the fragility of detente, precisely because it is an effort to transcend (not a means of eliminating) an underlying adversary relationship. It is their belief in the possibility of cooperation, their fear lest it break down and their sense of the importance of maintaining it which generate their policy toward the Middle East. They do not want events in this region (or any other) to give rise to a new spiral of mutual mistrust, and they want to limit the superpowers' involvement and commitments in the area so as to prevent political, as well as military, confrontation between them. Ideally, they would like to see an explicit agreement between the U.S. and the USSR, specifying the activities in which each could engage. They by no means want the USSR to withdraw from the region and leave it to its adversary, but they do not want its presence there to cause needless suspicion or alarm. Most of all they want to de-escalate (although not eliminate) the conflict between their own Middle East allies on the one hand, and the ally of the United States on the other, and they therefore support a political agreement between the two sides. They view the Israeli–Palestinian conflict as the chief obstacle to an agreement. That is why they vigorously defend the need to implement the rights of the Palestinians (not out of an intrinsic interest in them as valuable allies). The issue of borders they see as less intractable, and they are open to the idea of "correcting" Israel's 1967 borders to make them more secure.

It is of sufficient importance to these who hold these views to see the intensity of the Middle East conflict reduced that they may be willing in the future to accept almost any means of accomplishing this, so long as the solution reached leaves the Soviets a role to play in the area. Even shuttle diplomacy, conducted exclusively by the United States, might conceivably be acceptable, provided the Soviet Union is adequately consulted as it proceeds and the arrangements made include a role for it. (If these conditions are not met, then an all-American effort to reach a settlement is bound to arouse opposition from a group which fundamentally regards the United States as an adversary.) Far preferable is a joint Soviet–American approach to a settlement, with the parties meeting under the joint auspices of the two superpowers, and arriving at an agreement that would be guaranteed by both.

Those who want to cooperate with the United States in reducing international tensions would probably like to limit the sale of arms, particularly offensive arms to the Middle East. But they could support such a plan only in the wake of a peace agreement, and only if other potential arms sellers also committed themselves to it. Only under such circumstances could they defend a proposal of this sort to internal groups who hold different views of the United States and Russia's relationship with it.

2) realistic competitor

This view of U.S.-Soviet relations is held by many state officials, including Premier Kosygin, who are concerned with economic, technical or purely administrative affairs. It is expressed in *Izvestiya*. As its name suggests, this approach to Soviet–American relations is based on a view of the United States (and the entire capitalist system) less as a partner than as a competitor, a rival against whom the USSR is engaged in an economic contest. Each participant believes his performance in the race will demonstrate the superiority of his own system, and this is an ultimate objective of each. But this is a distant goal. In the interim, each sees that an economic and technological relationship with the other will improve his performance. Those who subscribe to this view may actually believe that the Soviet Union has more to gain than the United States from such a relationship. But if so, they do not acknowledge this. Their public position is simply that there is mutual benefit to be gained, that development of relations with the other is in the interest of each and that influential groups in both countries realize this. If, as the race proceeds, their competitor should weaken and fall behind (as ultimately he must), this would be a welcome development. But at the moment the USSR should not seek direct methods to bring this about, but should concentrate instead on cultivating economic ties with its rival. At the present time the highest priority for the Soviet Union in its relations with the United States should be the acquisition of American technology and investment capital on favorable terms.

This, for those who regard the United States as a competitor, is the chief rationale for detente. Relaxation of international tensions will create a climate of opinion in both countries favorable to economic and technological exchange.

As detente serves an extremely important purpose, it is important to cultivate and protect it. But one need not take extreme measures in this direction: one's competitor has an equally large stake in preserving it. In the Middle East it is desirable to find a political solution to the Arab–Israeli conflict because the periodic eruption of violence there is not conducive to the relaxation of international tensions. If, however, the Arabs use the period before a settlement is reached to apply economic pressure against the United States, that is all to the good. Indeed, they should be encouraged to maintain that pressure even after a peace agreement.

It is not the responsibility of economic executives and technocrats to concern themselves with political conflicts in every corner of the globe, particularly with the aims and activities of non-governmental groups. One senses a reluctance among those who hold this set of views to become involved in the question of the terms on which the Arab–Israeli dispute might be settled. The "legitimate" rights and security needs of parties ought obviously to be taken into account. The territorial arrangements and political status which may or may not be accorded various groups in the area are not of great interest.

Those who view the United States as an economic rival are not likely to favor limitation of arms sales, now that the Arabs have the wherewithal to pay for them. This is particularly true as those payments would be made in hard currency, which the Soviet Union could then use in the West. Moreover, arms technology is one of the few areas in which the Soviet Union could successfully compete with the West. It would thus be all the more imperative for Russia to continue to sell the Arabs arms, and especially advanced offensive weapons which Western governments might be hesitant to offer. If those who regard Soviet–American relations as competitive were to urge such a policy, they would be likely to find support among those who hold the third of the four basic views of this relationship.

3) unalterable antagonist

The third basic approach to the United States is to regard it as a dangerous and inexorably hostile antagonist, whose economic and military power are a grave threat to the USSR. This view, shared by groups within the military, ideologists and controllers (police, youth leaders and trade union officials), is reflected in *Krasnaya Zvezda, Komsomolskaya Pravda* and *Trud.* Those who hold this outlook believe the United States must be countered and contained, both militarliy and politically. It is thus of the highest priority, in their eyes, to expand Soviet military power and political influence on a global scale. The

USSR must acquire friends and military facilities wherever these will aid it in containing or undermining American power. It must also maintain a high level of domestic vigilance to counter American efforts to conduct ideological and political subversion. Although some segments of the military nay regard arms limitation as a desirable consequence of detente, all who subscribe to this approach to U.S.–Soviet relations view detente first and foremost as an American scheme to distract or lure Soviet officials and citizens into lowering their guard. Insofar as its avowed aim is the reduction of international tensions, it is dangerous illusion. The United States has no intention of altering its aggressive policy toward the Soviet Union, and thus the tension in Soviet–American relations must persist.

Those who think in these terms would obviously not be excessively dismayed, and would probably be generally relieved if events in the Middle East were to disrupt detente. Then the inevitable antagonism between the United States and the Soviet Union could be openly and fully discussed, and Soviet citizens adequately trained to recognize and cope with it.

Their vision of the future of Soviet–American relations thus gives this group no incentive to seek a settlement of the Arab–Israeli dispute. Quite the contrary. If it can be kept alive, it may provide a useful obstacle to the development of detente, just as the Vietnam War did in its time. With the Middle East conflict unresolved, Soviet aid will be eagerly sought, thus enabling the USSR to obtain naval and air-landing facilities in the area. And just as a dangerous Chinese–American alliance was impossible while the fighting continued in Vietnam, so undesirable Arab–American links will be impeded while the tension remains high in the West Bank, the Sinai and the Golan. If American attention and resources are absorbed there, it should hardly be regretted in Moscow. (The drain on Soviet resources does not seem to worry those who think along these lines.) Instead of fearing a Soviet–American military confrontation in the event of war, this group actually may welcome another outbreak of fighting: it would be an excellent opportunity to show the Pentagon what Soviet weapons and training can do — even in the hands of illiterate peasants.

As one might expect, this group does not have a plan for peace — at least not one it believes could be adopted without a radical change in Israeli society. Insofar as they support the idea of a settlement at all, it is under conditions which would substantially weaken American influence in the area. One might contemplate a peace settlement between, on the one hand, an Israel, reduced to the borders the United Nations allotted to it in 1947, incorporating a large population of Palestinian Arab "returnees," and, on the other hand, the Arab states, possibly including a Palestinian state. (The interest some members of this group display in the Palestinians is probably in part a result of the Palestinians' poor relations with the United States at the time of the October War.) Those who view the United States as a dangerous antagonist can only view shuttle diplomacy with suspicion. Insofar as they see anything to be gained from any other efforts to resolve the conflict, it is the possibility that Israeli intransigence manifested in the course of such efforts will harm Arab–American relations.

4)   mitigable opponent

One set of views expressed in the Soviet press is not based on any one of these images alone, but rather on a combination of two of them. These are the opinions of Russian nationalists, expressed in *Sovetskaya Rossiya*. The attitude of this group toward the United States and toward Soviet–American relations is ambivalent. Its members regard America as an antagonist, but not with the same sense of inevitability as one finds among the military, the ideologues and the controllers. The view expressed by the nationalists is that while the United States harbors aggressive aspirations against the Soviet Union, it can be moved to restrain its ambitions for the sake of its own security. Their image of Soviet–American relations is thus buttressed both by an awareness of the danger if the antagonism between the two opponents is not curbed and by the belief that it can be. Hence one finds in this group a warmer attitude toward detente and less skepticism as to its attainability. As these Russian nationalists are fiercely proud of the Soviet Union and Soviet achievements, they may be flattered by American recognition of the USSR as a partner in the management of the international system. Perhaps for this reason, too, they are willing to give detente a chance.

As this group sees it, the power of Zionist forces in American politics constitutes nearly as much danger to the USSR as the economic and military strength of the United States. These Russian nationalists stand in great awe of the international Zionist movement. They thus prefer a political solution to a perpetuation of the Arab–Israeli conflict in its present form. A de-escalation of the Arab–Israeli dispute would not merely enable the USSR to give detente a fair trial, a better chance to develop it into a permanent relationship. It would also reduce the influence of Zionism on American policy-makers and deflect Zionist enmity away from the Soviet Union. Possibly they are happy with the idea of a sizeable Zionist-inspired Jewish emigration from the USSR, which would decrease Zionist influence there, but which could only be allowed after the Arabs had ended their state of war with Israel. At any rate, they do support a settlement, albeit with less ardor than those who anticipate a more positive, cooperative relationship with the American adversary.

SOVIET POLITICS AND SOVIET POLICY
IN THE MIDDLE EAST

In conclusion we might consider the implications of these findings both for our understanding of Soviet politics and our expectations regarding the future course of Soviet policy in the Middle East. What, first of all, do they tell us about political alliances and alignments in the Soviet Union? And what will be the key factors shaping Soviet Middle Eastern policy in the next few years?

70

One interesting result to emerge from this study is that it offers no evidence of a military-industrial alliance of the kind often supposed to exist in the USSR in particular and in powerful industrial societies in general. Of course the absence of evidence is in this case not sufficient to prove the absence of the phenomenon. *Izvetiya* simply may not reflect the full range of foreign policy views to be found among industrial managers, planners and administrators, and *Krasnaya Zvezda* may be similarly limited as an indicator of military opinions. Still, it is worth noting that what does emerge is a striking dissimilarity between the foreign policy views of captains of industry and commanders of troops (or more accurately, between those responsible for economic administration and managers of the defense establishment). Apparently the lure of American technology has been able to weaken the natural ties between heavy industry (which dominates the industrial sector as a whole) and the military. A similar parting of ways occurred in the United States during the Vietnam War, when many corporations were anxious to reduce production of relatively unprofitable military hardware. Perhaps Schumpeter's observation that producers prefer peace[207] is system-invariant.

A second interesting finding is that there seems to be a close congruence of views between the military, or some segments of it, and ideologists. This is noteworthy because it is usually assumed that the relationship between these two groups is primarily one of tension and mutual resentment.[208] Students of Party–Army relations have generally concluded that the two groups are political rivals, each desiring to curb the power of the other. This study suggests that they have strong reason to cooperate, and probably do so — not merely in foreign policy debates, but also in selection of personnel for policy-making posts.

It is also worthy of note that Russian nationalists do not appear to be strong supporters of the views of the military. Once again it is possible that the newspaper studied does not accurately reflect the views of the group with which it is associated. But it is also possible that the challenge of survival in a nuclear age has had a moderating influence on traditionally militaristic groups, thus disrupting a political alliance which prevailed for centuries.

Finally, it is significant that a pragmatic, flexible approach to foreign policy seems to characterize not merely technocrats and government administrators, but also Party officials — unless, of course, *Pravda* speaks only for Brezhnev and not for a larger group with a career pattern similar to his. If, as this study of *Pravda* and *Izvestiya* seems to suggest, there really has emerged on the Soviet political scene a pro-detente alliance of industrial managers and apparatchiki, this would be one of the most important developments in Soviet politics in the last devade, a worthy subject of study in its own right. Even if such an alliance failed to incorporate many members of each of these groups, the very fact of its existence would have profound implications for the future course of Soviet foreign policy. Neither one of these groups has tended in the past to exert a moderating influence on Soviet policy toward the West. In fact, opposition to detente from both these quarters was important in shaping Khrushchev's foreign policy throughout most of the years of his leadership and Brezhnev's policy in the period immediately after he replaced Khrushchev. It may, indeed, have been one of the reasons for Khrushchev's downfall.[209]

We cannot predict the specific character of future Soviet policy toward the West and the Middle East on the basis of these findings. What we can do is suggest some of the important factors or forces which will influence it. So long as Brezhnev and Kosygin remain in office, much will depend on their personal evaluations of the chances for and utility of detente, and on their ability to retain or increase support for this policy within the Party and government. Brezhnev's ability, too, to continue to obtain the backing of Russian nationalist elements, both for him personally and for his foreign policy, will be of some significance. But even if this pro-detente alliance persists, the most important question is whether it will continue to be strong enough to overcome the opposing alliance of military leaders, ideologues and controllers, who consider the attempt to reduce international tensions to be either pernicious or doomed to fail. The possibility of strategic arms limitation and of political divisions in the Western alliance, encouraged by detente, may be sufficiently appealing to members of these groups so as to induce some of them to accept this policy. Whether it will also incline them to accept a peace settlement in the Middle East is more dubious.

Beyond the most immediate future lies the question of the next succession struggle and its relationship to these issues. In each of the two post-Stalin successions, the successful contender attained and consolidated his position in part by adopting a hard line in East–West relations — a line which appealed at the time not merely to Party apparachiki and industrial managers, but also to the military and professional ideologues. The nature of Soviet foreign policy in the next few years may well depend on whether or not the unity of views among these groups re-emerges. If it does, Brezhnev's successor will find it politically necessary, regardless of his personal views, to abandon detente. If it does not, and if the West remains interested, the newly appointed General Secretary may break with tradition and continue the pursuit of political cooperation and economic exchange with the West. The likelihood of future Soviet support for a Middle East peace settlement will in turn depend in large part on which of these two developments occurs.

NOTES

1. Theodore Draper, *Israel and World Politics* (New York: The Viking Press, 1968); Nadav Safran, *From War to War* (New York: Western Publishing Company, Inc., 1969); Aaron S. Klieman, *Soviet Russia and the Middle East* (Baltimore: Johns Hopkins Press, 1970); Roman Kolkowicz, "The Soviet Policy in the Middle East," in *The USSR and the Middle East* ed. by Michael Confino and Shimon Shamir (Jerusalem: Israel Universities Press, 1973); Adam Ulam, *Expansion and Coexistence* (New York: Praeger Publishers, 1974).

2. Walter Laqueur, *The Soviet Union and the Middle East* (London: Routledge and Kegan Paul, 1959); Arnold Horelick, "Soviet Policy in the Middle East," in *Political Dynamics in the Middle East,* ed. by Paul Y. Hammond and Sidney S. Alexander (New York: American Elsevier Publishing Company, Inc., 1972); Walter Laqueur, *The Struggle for the Middle East* (Harmondsworth, Middlesex: Penguin Books, 1972); Lincoln Landis, *Politics and Oil* (New York: Dunellen Publishing Company, 1973); Charles McLane, *Soviet–Middle East Relations* (London: Central Asian Research Centre, 1973): Foy D. Kohler, Leon Gouré, and Mose L. Harvey, *The Soviet Union and the October 1973 Middle East War* (Coral Gables: Center for Advanced International Studies, University of Miami, 1974); Robert O. Freedman, *Soviet Policy Toward the Middle East Since 1970* (New York: Praeger Publishers, 1975); Galia Golan, *Yom Kippur and After: The Soviet Union and the Middle East Crisis* (Cambridge, England: Cambridge University Press, 1976).

3. John C. Campbell, "The Communist Powers and the Middle East: Moscow's Purposes," *Problems of Communism* (Sept.–Oct. 1972).

4. Thomas W. Wolfe, "The Soviet Quest for More Globally Mobile Military Power," Memo, RM-5554-PR (Santa Monica: RAND, 1967); Thomas W. Wolfe, *Soviet Power and Europe* (Baltimore: The Johns Hopkins Press, 1970); Abraham S. Becker, "Oil and the Persian Gulf in Soviet Policy in the 1970's," in Confino and Shamir, eds., *The USSR and the Middle East:* Gur Ofer, "The Economic Burden of Soviet

Involvement in the Middle East," in Confino and Shamir, eds., *The USSR and the Middle East.*

5. Alexander Dallin, "Domestic Factors Influencing Soviet Foreign Policy," in Confino and Shamir, eds., *The USSR and the Middle East.*

6. Thomas Perry Thornton, *The Third World in Soviet Perspective* (Princeton: Princeton University Press, 1964); George Lenczowski, *Soviet Advances in the Middle East* (Washington: American Enterprise Institute for Public Policy Research, 1971); Aryeh Yodfat, *Arab Politics in the Soviet Mirror* (Jerusalem: Israel Universities Press, 1973); Roger Kanet, "Soviet Attitudes Toward Developing Nations Since Stalin," in *The Soviet Union and the Developing Nations* (Baltimore: Johns Hopkins, 1974).

7. Robert C. Tucker, *The Soviet Political Mind* (revised edition; New York: W.W. Norton and Company, Inc., 1971).

8. Uri Ra'anan, *The USSR Arms the Third World* (Cambridge, Mass.: The MIT Press, 1969); Galia Golan, "Internal Pressures and Soviet Fpreign Policy Decisions," (Jerusalem: 1973; unpublished paper); Ilana Dimant-Kass, "*Pravda* and *Trud* — Divergent Attitudes Toward the Middle East," *Soviet Union* (Winter, 1974); Ilana Dimant-Kass, "The Soviet Military and Soviet Policy in the Middle East 1970–1973," *Soviet Studies*, XXVI (October, 1974); Avraham Ben-Tsur, *Soviet Factors and the Six-Day War* (Tel Aviv: Sifriat Poalim, 1975: in Hebrew).

9. For discussion of internal influences on Soviet foreign policy, see John A. Armstrong, "The Domestic Roots of Soviet Foreign Policy," *International Affairs*, XLI (January, 1965); Vernon Aspaturian, "Internal Politics and Foreign Policy in the Soviet System," in *Approaches to Comparative and International Politics*, ed. by R. Barry Farrell (Evanston: Northwestern University Press, 1966); Sidney I. Ploss, "Studying the Domestic Determinants of Soviet Foreign Policy," *Canadian Slavic Studies*, I (Spring, 1967); Philip Windsor and Adam Roberts, *Czechoslovakia, 1968* (London: Chatto and Windus, 1969); David W. Paul, "Soviet Foreign Policy and the Invasion of Czechoslovakia," *International Studies Quarterly*, IV (June, 1971).

10. For an exposition of these ideas see Zbigniew Brzezinski, *Ideology and Power in Soviet Politics* (New York: Praeger Publishers, 1962); Carl Friedrich and Zbigniew Brzezinski, *Totalitarian Dictatorship and Autocracy* (Cambridge: Harvard University Press, 1956); Merle Fainsod, *How Russia Is Ruled* (Revised edition; Cambridge: Harvard

University Press, 1965); Robert Daniels, "Doctrine and Foreign Policy," *Survey* 57 (October, 1965); William Zimmerman, "Elite Perspectives and the Explanation of Soviet Foreign Policy," *Journal of International Affairs*, XXIV, No. 1 (1970). Also see the place Rosenau accords "societal" variables in closed systems. (James Rosenau, "Pre-Theories and Theories of Foreign Policy," in *The Scientific Study of Foreign Policy* [New York: The Free Press, 1971].)

11. But see Allen Kassof, "The Administered Society: Totalitarianism Without Terror," *World Politics* XVI (July, 1964); T. H. Rigby, "Traditional, Market and Organizational Societies and the USSR," *Ibid.*; Marchal Shulman, *Beyond the Cold War* (New Haven: Yale University Press, 1966); Carl Friedrich, "The Evolving Theory and Practice of Totalitarian Regimes," in *Totalitarianism in Perspective*, ed. by Friedrich, Michael Curtis and Benjamin Barber (New York: Praeger, 1969).

12. Consider the following statements by students of Soviet foreign policy (all of whom have written on Soviet policy in the Middle East):

"To begin with, the concept 'domestic politics' has only a very limited applicability in the Soviet Union. The country has neither political parties nor an articulate public opinion. Control by the government since the 1930's of virtually all the productive wealth of the country means that economic forces cannot function as a separate factor in the country's political life."

"...the student of both Tsarist and Soviet history is struck by the insignificant influence that public opinion and the pressure of domestic politics have exercised on the conduct of Russian foreign policy." (Richard Pipes, "Domestic Politics and Foreign Affairs," in *Russian Foreign Policy: Essays in Historical Perspective*, ed. by Ivo Lederer [New Haven: Yale University Press, 1962], pp. 161, 168).

Pipes points out that the elimination of domestic politics in the USSR has given the Soviet state a flexibility in foreign policy "which no democratic state can match." (*Ibid.*, p. 169).

Ulam draws a similar conclusion. Commenting on Soviet policy during the October, 1973 war in the Middle East, he writes, "The above story provides a vivid demonstration of how, for all the extent of the Soviet Union's involvement in the Middle East, the character of the Soviet regime provides it with a degree of maneuverability and flexibility that the United States cannot enjoy in similar situations. To a degree it can operate clandestinely: how many Soviet citizens are even now aware that in 1970 some Russian pilots were shot down in air fights over the Suez Canal? It is impossible for the Soviet consumer to arrive at a precise calculation of how far his privations are related to the expense his government incurs in arming the progressive Arab states..." (Adam Ulam, *Expansion and Co-existence*, p. 760).

Horelick and Rush likewise emphasize the importance of the Soviet leadership's tight control over communication media in the nuclear age. They stress that the Soviet public has no significant influence on Soviet foreign policy — in comparison with the influence groups, parties and peoples in the West can have on their governments' foreign policies. (Arnold Horelick and Myron Rush, *Strategic Power and Soviet Foreign Policy* [Chicago: University of Chicago Press, 1966].)

13. C. Grant Pendill, Jr. in "Bipartisanship in Soviet Foreign Policy Making" sought to elucidate the impact of factional struggles on Soviet foreign policy under Khrushchev. He found he could not substantiate the hypothesis that these struggles yielded conflicts of opinion which affected foreign policy. (Erik P. Hoffman and Frederic J. Fleron, Jr., eds., *The Conduct of Soviet Foreign Policy* [London: Butterworths, 1971].)

The relative dearth of evidence of divergent views on foreign, as compared to domestic, policy may explain why the totalitarian model has not been as readily or as widely repudiated by students of the Soviets' external conduct.

14. Sidney Ploss, "New Politics in Russia," *Survey* XIX (Autumn, 1973).

15. *Sovetskaya Rossiya* [hereafter abbreviated SR], Oct. 9, 11, 16, 1973.

16. *Pravda*, Oct. 8, 9, 11, 12, 17, 19, 1973.

17. *Izvestiya* [hereafter abbreviated IZ], Oct. 11, 13, 1973. Emphasis mine.

18. The problem of interpretation is complicated by the fact that one rarely finds complete consistency. *Pravda* and *Sovetskaya Rossiya* on one occasion use the same formula as *Izvestiya* (October 13, 1973). This may suggest general agreement among the three papers. Alternatively, the agreement might be confined to the occasion. The "Israel alone" formula appeared in these three papers immediately

after Israel sank the Soviet merchant ship, the Ilya Mechnikov, in a Syrian harbor. On this particular occasion all major Soviet newspapers were probably instructed to distinguish clearly between Israeli and American actions. This would help forestall demands or expectations that the USSR would take retaliatory measures against the United States.

19. *Pravda*, Oct. 19, 1973.

20. *Pravda*, Oct. 19, 1973.

21. This problem is discussed by Golan, "Internal Pressures."

22. Leonid Vladimirov, *The Russians* (New York: Prageer, 1968), pp. 79–107; Hedrick Smith, "In Moscow, the Bigger the News, the Smaller the Story," *New York Times Magazine*, Nov. 23, 1975.

23. One of the most serious accusations the Chinese have levelled against the Soviets is that they made public the existence of the Sino–Soviet dispute. "To lay bare a dispute between fraternal parties or fraternal countries openly in the face of the enemy cannot be regarded as a serious Marxist–Leninist attitude. Such an attitude will only grieve those near and dear to us and gladden our enemies." Speech by Chou En-lai to the Twenty-second Congress of the Communist Party of the Soviet Union, Oct. 19, 1961. Printed in David Floyd, *Mao Against Khrushchev* (New York: Praeger, 1963), p. 316.

24. Nathan Leites, *A Study of Bolshevism* (Glencoe: Free Press, 1953); Alfred G. Meyer, *Leninism* (Cambridge: Harvard University Press, 1957). See also Howard Biddulph, "Protest Strategies of the Soviet Intellectual Opposition," in Rudolf L. Tökés, ed., *Dissent in the U.S.S.R.* (Baltimore: Johns Hopkins, 1975).

25. Leites, *A Study of Bolshevism.*

26. There is some recent evidence that the Soviet leadership has come to realize that there are diplomatic benefits to be gained by a display of internal differences. General Secretary Brezhnev apparently discovered Mr. Kissinger's sympathy for statesmen who operate under internal pressures. On several occasions he left the American Secretary of State with the clear impression that his policies were sharply opposed by other Politburo members and several powerful political groups. This made Kissinger all the more eager to support and conciliate the General Secretary. (Helmut Sonnenfeldt, speech delivered at the Center for International Relations, Harvard University, Spring, 1974.) From all we know, however, these differences were genuine.

27. *Pravda*, Oct. 18, 1973; *Izvestiya*, Oct. 20, 1973.

28. Robert Conquest, *Power and Policy in the USSR* (New York: St. Martin's Press, 1961); Sidney I. Ploss, *Conflict and Decision-Making in Soviet Russia* (Princeton: Princeton University Press, 1965); Carl Linden, *Khrushchev and the Soviet Leadership* (Baltimore: Johns Hopkins Press, 1966); Alexander Dallin and Alan F. Westin, eds., *Politics in the Soviet Union* (New York: Harcourt, Brace and World, 1966); Michel Tatu, *Power in the Kremlin* (New York: Viking, 1969); Sidney I. Ploss, ed., *The Soviet Political Process* (Waltham: Ginn and Company, 1971).

29. James Rosenau argues that "role" variables are the most significant of the factors influencing foreign policy-making in industrialized (hence bureaucratic) societies. (Rosenau, "Pre-theories and Theories of Foreign Policy," pp. 112–113.)

30. Jeremy Azrael, *Managerial Power and Soviet Politics* (Cambridge: Harvard University Press, 1964); Roman Kolkowicz, *The Soviet Military and the Communist Party* (Princeton: Princeton University Press, 1967); P. H. Juviler and H. W. Morton, eds., *Soviet Policy-Making: Studies of Communism in Transition* (New York: Praeger, 1967); Joel J. Schwartz and William R. Keech, "Group Influence on the Policy Process in the Soviet Union," *APSR*, LXII (Sept., 1968) 840–851; Sidney Ploss, "Interest Groups," in Allen Kassof, ed., *Prospects for Soviet Society* (New York: Praeger, 1968, pp. 76–103; Phillip Stewart, "Soviet Interest Groups and the Policy Process," *World Politics*, XXII (October, 1969), pp. 29–50; H. Gordon Skilling and Franklyn Griffiths, eds., *Interest Groups in Soviet Politics* (Princeton: Princeton University Press, 1971); Donald R. Kelley, "Interest Groups in the USSR," *Journal of Politics*, XXXIV (August, 1972) 860–88; Theodore H. Friedgut, "Interest Groups in Soviet Policy-Making: The MTS Reforms," Research Paper No. 12 (Jerusalem: The Soviet and East European Research Centre, Hebrew University, 1975).

31. See for example Robert Slusser, "Khrushchev, China, and the Hydra-Headed Opposition," in Juliver and Morton, eds., *Soviet Policy Making*; Wolfgang Leonhard, "The Domestic Politics of the New Soviet Foreign Policy," *Foreign Affairs*, LII (October, 1973).

32. Warren E. Miller and Donald E. Stokes, "Constituency Influence in Congress," *American Political Science Review*, LVII (March, 1963), 45–56; Douglas A. Chalmers, *The SPD: From Working Class Movement to Modern Political Party* (New Haven: Yale University Press, 1964); Herbert J. Spiro, "Comparative Politics: A Comprehensive

Approach," *American Political Science Review*, LVI (September, 1962), 577–595; Aaron Wildavsky, "The Analysis of Issue Contexts in the Study od Decision-Making," *Journal of Politics*, 24 (Nov., 1962), 717–732. For an argument that in some respects foreign policy is itself a distinctive issue-area see James Rosenau, "Foreign Policy as an Issue-Area," in Rosenau, ed., *Domestic Sources of Foreign Policy* (New York: The Free Press, 1967) pp. 11–50.

33. Hassanein Heikal, *The Road to Ramadan* (London: Collins, 1975).

34. See note 8.

35. Mention should also be made of the excellent collection of materials on Soviet policy in the Middle East which was made available to the author by the Soviet and East European Research Centre of the Hebrew University.

36. Two salient examples are the year and a half preceding the "anti-party crisis" of June, 1957, and the year following Khrushchev's removal in October, 1964. In the first of these periods Khrushchev was struggling to attain a pre-eminent position in the Presidium and courted "liberal" opinion. Thus groups advocating internal liberalization were able to win acceptance of a wide range of "destalinizing" measures: extension of amnesty provisions to a large number of political prisoners, rehabilitation of some of Stalin's victims, reform of the criminal code and the code of criminal procedure, relaxation of censorship and removal of the nearly complete ban imposed by Stalin on foreign travel and contacts with foreigners. In the latter period Brezhnev was engaged in a similar struggle and likewise courted certain political elite groups (in this case "conservatives"). Thus groups opposed to Khrushchev's policies were able to have many of them withdrawn or amended. They won a revocation of Khrushchev's administrative reorganizations, a halt to denunciations of Stalin, a larger budget for the Party apparatus and changes in military policy.

37. An example is the year following the Twenty-second Party Congress in October, 1961. Khrushchev was attempting to strengthen his position, and liberals were again able to have an impact on policy (most notably on cultural policy).

38. Kunayev, Kulakov, Grishin and Shcherbitsky.

39. Golan, "Internal Pressures."

40. Brzezinski, *Ideology and Power*, pp. 102–113; Zbigniew Brzezinski

and Samuel P. Huntington, *Political Power USA/USSR* (New York: The Viking Press, 1963), pp. 56–70.

41. Franklyn Griffiths, "A Tendency Analysis of Soviet Policy-Making," in Skilling and Griffiths, eds., *Interest Groups in Soviet Politics.*

42. Daniel Bell, "Ten Theories in Search of Reality," in *Soviet Conduct in World Affairs*, ed. by Alexander Dallin (New York: Columbia University Press, 1960), pp. 25–26.

43. A position in the Middle East is of greater value and importance to the navy than to the air force, whose operations are hampered as well as facilitated by the Soviet presence there. The ground forces have little to gain from this presence. Dimant-Kass proposes that there may be two points of view on Soviet policy in the Middle East within the military, with the strategic forces and the military intelligence opposed to Soviet involvement in the region and the theater forces in favor of it. (Dimant-Kass, "The Soviet Military and Soviet Policy in the Middle East," 520–21).

44. The organs associated with the navy and the MPA (the organization of "political commanders" and political instructors in the armed forces), *Morskoi Sbornik* and *Kommunist Vooruzhennykh Sil*, did not distinguish themselves from *Krasnaya Zvezda* on the subject of the Middle East. One can thus assume that Grechko's views coincided with those of the heads of these institutions, Admiral Gorshkov and Marshal Epishev, respectively.

45. The author sought, but could not find, newspapers which both commented on the Middle East on a regular basis and which could be identified as distinctive spokesmen for either economists, consumers, enterprise managers in light industry, or managers in heavy and defense industries. *Voprosy Ekonomiki, Ekonomicheskaya Gazeta* and *Foreign Trade* represent the views of economists and managers, but they had little to say on the Middle East and could not be clearly associated with light or heavy industry. As in many capitalist countries, consumers have no regular outlet in the media (although *Krokodil and Literaturnaya Gazeta* sometimes champion their interests).

46. *Pravda*, Oct. 7, 1973.

47. *Pravda*, Oct. 19, 1973.

48. *Pravda*, Oct. 19, 1973.

49. *Pravda*, Oct. 14, 1973. *Izvestiya* carries the same quote (Oct. 14, 1973).

50. *Pravda*, Oct. 9, 10, 11, 14, 16, 17, 18, 1973.

51. *Pravda*, Oct. 14, 16, 22, 1973.

52. All the major Soviet newspapers hold Israel responsible for the outbreak of war. But only *Pravda* repeatedly refers to numerous occasions on which a peaceful settlement could have been reached had *Israel* not blocked it. (Oct. 8, 12, 14, 16, 17, 1973.)

53. For example, *Pravda*'s version of the major wartime speech by Syrian President Assad omit his denunciation of "those who aid Israel in its aggression." The version carried by *SR*, *Trud* and *IZ* includes this attack. (Oct. 17, 1973.) On the same day *Krasnaya Zvezda* reports a Tunisian protest against American aid to the Arabs' enemy; *Pravda* does not mention this protest.

54. See *SR* and *Trud*, Oct. 11, 1973, and *Krasnaya Zvezda* (hereafter abbreviated *KZ*), *SR*, *Trud* and *IZ*, Oct. 16, 1973.

55. *Pravda*, Oct. 8, 12, 17, 1973.

56. All the major papers strongly condemn the bombing. *Pravda* gives more detail about its economic consequences. it quotes the Syrian Minister of Planning to the effect that Israel is trying to destroy the basis of the Syrian economy — its plants, ports, oil refineries and power stations. (*Pravda*, Oct. 13, 1973.)

57. *Pravda* prints the warning by Israel's Deputy Primier Allon that Israel will not stop at the 1967 cease-fire lines, reports Israeli penetration of those lines and repeatedly describes Israel as "expansionist" and "annexationist." (*Pravda*, Oct. 11, 12, 13, 14, 17, 1973.)

58. *Pravda*, Oct. 7, 8, 11, 13, 1973.

59. *Pravda*, Oct. 12, 13, 14, 17, 18, 20, 21, 1973.

60. On Oct. 11, 1973, *Pravda* carries, but does not comment on, a TASS report that the parliamentary fraction of the Israeli Communist Party has demanded immediate discussion of its cease-fire proposal. When *Pravda* reports an action or resolution of a foreign Communist party, it usually means that the Soviet Party leaders or a powerful faction within the Soviet Party approved of the measure.
On Oct. 12, 1973, in another TASS report, *Pravda* quotes the French newspaper *Figaro* as saying that "the success achieved by the Arab countries in the first days of the war is quite sufficient to make Israel understand that the times have changed." *Pravda* may thus be signalling its or Brezhnev's conviction that enough has been accomplished on the battlefield, and it is time to silence the guns. (See the discussion of this point in Golan, *The Soviet Union and the Yom Kippur War*.)

61. For an argument that this was, indeed, Brezhnev's wish, see Golan, *The Soviet Union and the Yom Kippur War.*

62. *Pravda,* Oct. 12, 14, 17, 1973.

63. *Pravda,* Oct. 9, 10, 11, 14, 15, 17, 18, 1973.

64. *Pravda,* Oct. 8, 18, 19, 22, 1973.

65. *Pravda,* Oct. 8, 1973.

66. This is the optimistic characterization of Egypt, Syria, Iraq, Algeria and the People's Democratic Republic of Yemen offered by the statement of the Conference of Arab Communist and Workers' Parties excerpted and summarized by *Pravda* (Oct. 19, 1973).

67. *Pravda* complains that Israel wants to control these resources (Oct. 13, 1973).

68. Over and over *Pravda* lashes out against Zionism, Zionists and "Zionist circles" and their aggressive aims and unprincipled methods (Oct. 8, 9, 12, 14, 17, 18, 19, 1973).

69. *Pravda,* Oct. 9, 10, 11, 12, 14, 16, 18, 21, 1973. Only *Izvestiya* evinces somewhat comparable interest in this goal.

70. *Pravda* notes the "justifiable concern" over this prospect on the part of many delegates to the United Nations (Oct. 18, 1973).

71. *Pravda,* Oct. 12, 1973.

72. *Pravda,* Oct. 21, 1973.

73. *Pravda,* Oct. 9, 1973. Brezhnev emphasized this in his first major speech after the war broke out. "Political circles and the broad masses of people in many countries increasingly realize," he told visiting Japanese Premier Tanaka, "that it is unacceptable and inadmissable that international differences and disputes should be resolved by military means." (*Pravda,* Oct. 9, 1973.)

74. The official Soviet government statement on the war, issued on Oct. 7, 1973, makes no reference to such an objective. Brezhnev personally broaches the subject the next day, at a luncheon in Tanaka's honor. (*Pravda,* Oct. 9, 1973.)

75. *Pravda,* Oct. 9, 10, 11, 12, 14, 16, 21, 1973. The other major Soviet papers (with the exception of *Izvestiya*) only mention this idea when they must print a Brezhnev speech or statement in which it is articulated. *Izvestiya* displays somewhat similar interest in this proposal.

76. *Pravda,* Oct. 7, 9, 10, 11, 12, 13, 14, 17, 1973.

77. *Pravda* carries without comment an article by the Secretary General of the Israeli Communist Party, M. Vilner, which asserts that

the only possible solution to the Middle East conflict must include, among other things, "acknowledgement of the right of the State of Israel to sovereign existence." (Oct. 17, 1973.) *Pravda* would not print without a rebuttal views on an extremely important issue which diverged widely from those of its patron. Thus one may infer that this is the position of Brezhnev and his supporters in the Party apparatus.

78. *Pravda*, Oct. 8, 9, 12, 17, 18, 1973. Emphasis mine.

79. *Pravda*, Oct. 7, 9, 10, 11, 1973. This is the position enunciated by Brezhnev at the outset of the war in his speech at the Tanaka luncheon (*Pravda*, Oct. 9, 1973.) *Pravda* quotes this speech on many subsequent occasions.

It is true that on one occasion *Pravda* takes a quite different, even apparently contradictory position. This is on Oct. 21, 1973, after Israel has crossed the canal in force and begun the encirclement of the Egyptian Third Army, but has not announced its agreement to a cease-fire and withdrawal to the east bank of the canal. Brezhnev fears that the Israelis will try to establish themselves permanently on the west bank. They might even attempt to take Cairo. At the very least their presence on the west bank would pose a constant threat to the Egyptian capital. *Pravda* commentator Vsevolod Ovchinnikov now attacks the notion that Israel needs "secure" borders as "groundless" and "disastrous for Israel itself." His intention is probably to convey to the United States the necessity, from the Soviet point of view, of an Israeli pullback from Cairo and the canal. Israel's argument that it must obtain new borders for the sake of security must now be undermined, lest it be used (successfully) to justify to the Americans an Israeli postion astride the canal.

Pravda's harder line at this time may also constitute an attempt to mollify the Arabs, who are bound to be unhappy with the terms of the cease-fire, just negotiated in Moscow. The Soviets at first tried to hold out for a substantial Israeli withdrawal as a condition for the cease-fire, in accord with Arab demands. But Kissinger was firm on this score and the Soviets ultimately agreed to a cease-fire in place. This decision was communicated to Kissinger on Oct. 21. It was, therefore, probably taken the evening before, as the Oct. 21 edition of *Pravda* was being prepared. The Ovchinnikov editorial was probably written either in anticipation or as a result of this concession.

80. *Pravda*, Oct. 7, 12, 13, 14, 18, 1973. On one occasion, *Pravda* even specifies withdrawal from *"unlawfully* occupied territories," a

concept which virtually invites negotiation and compromise. (Oct. 13, 1973). Russian has no definite article, so it is impossible to say whether one should be inserted in these translations. The emphasis is mine.

81. *Pravda*, Oct. 8, 9, 12, 13, 14, 22, 1973.

82. *Pravda*, Oct. 10, 17, 19, 1973.

83. *Pravda*, Oct. 19, 1973. This is the statement issued by the Conference of Arab Communist and Workers' Parties.

84. *Pravda*, Oct. 10, 13, 15, 16, 18, 20, 22, 1973. On Oct. 18, 1973, the entire report by *Pravda*'s Middle East correspondent is devoted to Palestinian guerilla operations. This is extremely unusual for a Soviet newspaper. This interpretation would explain why the other newspaper most interested in the Palestinians is the one we would expect to be least sensitive to Chinese competition in the third world and the international Communist movement, and least inclined to believe that a national resistance movement had any claims on the USSR or could offer the Soviets anything of value. (This is *Izvestiya*.).

85. For the treatment of detente by *Izvestiya*, see Oct. 10, 11, 13, 18, 21, 24, 1973.

86. An *IZ* commentary on the Tanaka visit stresses the urgency of achieving a relaxation of international tensions and implementing "a stable and general peace." The article lauds the readiness of Japan and the USSR "to make a constructive contribution to the cause of further strengthening lasting peace and the security of all peoples" and notes that both sides advocate the "speediest implementation" of nuclear and also conventional disarmament.

87. *IZ*, Oct. 14, 1973.

88. *IZ*, Oct. 11, 1973.

89. *IZ*, Oct. 11, 14, 20, 21, 1973.

90. "The world is again faced with a dangerous development of events. The hotbed of bloody armed conflict in the Middle East is fraught with serious consequences for the international situation." (*IZ*, Oct. 11, 1973.)

91. In a report on the emergency session of the Presidential Group of the World Peace Council held in the first week of the war, *IZ* notes that this group called for sanctions against Israel. The *Pravda* account of the meeting omits this proposal. (*IZ*, Oct. 12, 1973; *Pravda*, Oct. 12, 1973.)

92. Although *Pravda* endorses the use of oil as a weapon in the struggle, it does not dwell on it. (See note 64.) *IZ* discourses at length

on its potential impact. (See text below and *IZ*, Oct. 16, 18, 19, 20, 21, 1973.)

93. *IZ* largely ignores those successes until Oct. 17, 1973. Compare the reporting of them in *Pravda*, as indicated in note 59. *IZ* does not carry either the Oct. 10 TASS report of the call for a cease-fire by the Israeli Communist Party or the *Figaro* assertion, reported in *Pravda* on Oct. 12, that the success achieved by the Arabs in the first days of the war is "quite sufficient." (See note 60.)

94. *IZ*, Oct. 21, 1973.

95. *IZ*, Oct. 13, 1973.

96. On the same day that *Pravda* first hints at the desirability of a cease-fire (see notes 60 and 93), *IZ* quotes the Egyptian Foreign Minister as telling the United Nations Security Council that Egypt will "do everything" to force Israel to cease bombing Arab territory. Unlike *Pravda*, which omits this threat in its account of the occasion, *IZ*, is evidently not concerned that such language might bring on greater American involvement in the war. (Compare "In the UN Security Council," *IZ*, Oct. 11, 1973 and *Pravda*, Oct. 11, 1973.)

97. *Pravda*, Oct. 18, 1973; *SR*, Oct. 18, 1973; *KP*, Oct. 18, 21, 1973.

98. *IZ*, Oct. 18, 20, 1973.

99. *IZ*, Oct. 20, 1973.

100. First the Syrian retreat, then the "deep penetration" of Israeli forces into Egyptian territory on the west bank of the canal. (*IZ*, Oct. 17, 21, 1973.)

101. *IZ*, Oct. 18, 1973.

102. *IZ*, Oct. 18, 1973.

103. Now even *Izvestiya* tries to persuade the Arabs that they have achieved enough and should accept a cease-fire. "However the present events in the Middle East may subsequently develop, they have already shown to the whole world that 1973 is not 1967..." (*IZ*, Oct. 19, 1973.)

104. *IZ*, Oct. 16, 18, 19, 20, 21, 1973.

105. *IZ*, Oct. 20, 1973.

106. *IZ*, Oct. 20, 1973. Translated in Foreign Broadcast Information Service, *Daily Report*, Oct. 24, 1973.

107. *IZ*, Oct. 20, 1973. Translated in FBIS, *Daily Report*, Oct. 24, 1973.

108. *IZ*, Oct. 20, 1973. Translated in FBIS, *Daily Report*, Oct. 24, 1973.

109. *IZ*, Oct. 20, 1973. Translated in FBIS, *Daily Report*, Oct. 24, 1973.

110. *IZ*, Oct. 19, 1973.

111. *IZ*, Oct. 10, 11, 12, 13, 14, 16, 19, 1973.

112. *IZ*, Oct. 9, 10, 11, 1973. On one occasion Israel's need for "secure borders" is given an intentionally restricted meaning. *IZ* commentator Kudriavtsev writes on Oct. 19, 1973, that Israel's stubborn insistence on readjusting her frontiers will bring it to catastrophe. Israel talks about "just and secure borders," Kudriavtsev continues. But what is just for the aggressor is not necessarily just for the victim of aggression, and security depends on one's relations with one's neighbors. Secure frontiers can be attained only when Israel establishes good neighborly relationswith the Arab states.

This departure from *IZ*'s main line was probably generated, like *Pravda*'s similar deviation (see note 79) by panic at Israel's presence on the west bank of the canal, less than a hundred miles from Cairo. Israel cannot, under any circumstances, be allowed to "readjust" her frontiers, as in 1967 and 1948, to correspond to the new positions of her army.

113. *IZ*, Oct. 11, 1973. *Izvestiya* joins *Pravda* in printing the demand of the Israeli Communist Party that the Arabs acknowledge "the right of the State of Israel to soverreign existence." (*IZ*, Oct. 18, 1973.)

114. *IZ*, Oct. 9, 19, 20, 1973.

115. *KZ*, Oct. 17, 1973. *KZ* also reprints important official documents and speeches which defend detente (Oct. 9, 11, 12, 17, 1973.)

116. Permanent relaxation of international tension is only possible on the basis of "the indestructable economic and defense might of the world's first worker-peasant state." Soviet commitment to peace entails "all-round support for the Arab peoples' liberation struggle." (*KZ*, Oct. 17, 1973.)

117. *KZ*, Oct. 9, 10, 11, 12, 17, 1973.

118. However, on one occasion, it does print a Brezhnev speech expressing such anxiety. (*KZ*, Oct. 9, 1973.)

119. *KZ*, Oct. 11, 1973.

120. *KZ*, Oct. 20, 1973.

121. *KZ*, Oct. 11, 12, 13, 14, 16, 17, 20, 1973. *Krasnaya Zvesda* is greatly relieved when the quality of Soviet weapons and the achievements of Soviet training programs begin to be noticed in the West and

frequently cites laudatory remarks on these matters from the Western press.

122. *KZ*, Oct. 17, 1973.

123. The language is that of the Soviet government statement issued on Oct. 7, 1973. *KZ* gives this portion of the statement particular emphasis. (*KZ*, Oct. 13, 1973.)

124. *KZ*, Oct. 9, 1973.

125. *KZ*, Oct. 9, 1973.

126. *KZ*, Oct. 13, 1973.

127. *KZ*, Oct. 16, 1973.

128. *KZ*, Oct. 16, 1973.

129. *KZ*, Oct. 16, 1973.

130. When the Middle East News Agency reports the beginning of preparations for clearing the canal and reopening it to navigation, *Pravda* ignores the dispatch, but *KZ*, like *IZ*, picks it up. The military organ notes that it is expected that the canal can be reopened in six months. (*KZ*, Oct. 19, 1973.)

131. In the five years prior to 1976 the USSR acquired naval and communications facilities in Somalia and air-landing rights in Kenya and established a military aid program, involving Russian advisors, in Somalia, Uganda and Mozambique. In the same period in West Africa the Soviets obtained naval- or air-landing rights in Mali, Guinea, Gabon, Nigeria and Angola. (*International Herald Tribune*, Jan. 30, 1976.)

132. Of the newspapers studied, only *SR* displays an interest in Africa similar to that of *Krasnaya Zvezda*. The treatment of a TASS dispatch is again indicative of *KZ*'s attitudes and concerns. On Oct. 13, 1973, TASS carried a list of the African states which had broken relations with Israel or condemned "Israeli aggression." Only *Krasnaya Zvezda* considers this newsworthy. (*KZ*, Oct. 14, 1973.) *KZ* is more interested than the other newspapers in Somalia's attitude toward the conflict in the Middle East. (Compare *KZ*'s version of an article entitled "Stop the Aggression!" which appeared on Oct. 16 with similar articles appearing in the other major newspapers on the same day.)

133. This is not mentioned in *KZ*. The Soviet press almost never refers to Soviet military facilities outside the Bloc or to any Soviet desire to obtain them. Only the capitalist countries entertain such imperialistic ambitions.

134. On the rare occasions when the phrase appears in *Krasnaya Zvezda*, it is almost always in a quotation of a speech or official document in which these words are used, rather than in an editorial or an article by one of the paper's own correspondents or staff writers. (*KZ*, Oct. 9, 11, 12, 14, 1973. Compare *Pravda* Oct. 9, 10, 11, 12, 14, 16, 18, 21, 1973, and *IZ*, Oct. 10, 11, 12, 13, 14, 16, 19, 1973.)

135. *Pravda*, Oct. 7, 8, 9, 10, 11, 13, 21, 22, 1973.

136. *Pravda*, Oct. 10, 1973; *IZ*, Oct. 10, 11, 1973.

137. *Pravda*, Oct. 10, 11, 18, 1973; *IZ*, Oct. 10, 1973.

138. *Pravda*, Oct. 9, 10, 11, 12, 14, 16, 21, 1973. *IZ* also supports the idea (Oct. 9, 10, 11, 12, 13, 16, 19, 1973.) *KZ* carries the Brezhnev speech proposing it (Oct. 9, 9173), the Soviet–Japanese joint statement, in which it is reiterated (Oct. 11, 1973) and a report of a Gromyko speech praising it (Oct. 12, 1973). Otherwise the military newspaper studiously ignores it.

139. *KZ*, Oct. 13, 1973.

140. *KZ*, Oct. 13, 1973.

141. *KZ* is also the only major Soviet newspaper which does not carry the Vilner statement, issued by the Israeli Communist Party. This statement calls for a solution to the Middle East conflict based on "observance of Security Council Resolution 242 and subsequent United Nations resolutions demanding implementation of a just and stable peace, on the basis of a withdrawal of Israeli troops from all the territories occupied in 1967 [and] the acknowledgement of the right of the State of Israel to sovereign existence." (*Pravda*, Oct. 17, 1973.)

142. *Pravda*, Oct. 7, 8, 9, 10, 11, 12, 17, 18, 1973; *IZ*, Oct. 9, 10, 11, 17, 1973.

143. *KZ*, Oct. 20, 1973.

144. *Pravda* does not actually employ these phrases, but it quotes a statement by the Lebanese Communist Party which does. (Oct. 10, 1973.) *Trud* is the only other major Soviet paper to carry this quote. (Oct. 10, 1973.) There is similar language on the report on the September, 1973, conference of the Arab Communist Parties, carried only by *Pravda*. (Oct. 19, 1973.)

145. *Pravda*, Oct. 8, 9, 11, 12, 14, 17, 19, 1973.

146. Occasionally they become "the Palestinian peoples." (*Pravda*, Oct. 13, 22, 1973.)

147. *IZ*, Oct. 9, 11, 17, 19, 22, 1973.

148. *KZ*, Oct. 9, 12, 13, 14, 16, 19, 1973.

149. *KZ* seems quite impressed by this alleged contribution of the Palestinians to the Arab war effort. It reports over a hundred sabotage operations on Israeli occupied territory in the first two weeks of the war, in addition to those conducted within the 1967 borders of the state. (Oct. 19, 1973.) However, as far as this author has been able to determine, these reports are wholly fictitious. One wonders about the quality of Soviet military intelligence and whether *KZ*'s editors had access to it.

150. *SR*, Oct. 18, 1973.

151. *SR*, Oct. 9, 1973. Compare the disscussion in *KZ*, Oct. 9, 1973.

152. *SR*, Oct. 8, 1973.

153. *SR*, Oct. 8, 9, 10, 17, 1973.

154. *SR*, Oct. 10, 1973.

155. *KZ* and *SR* describe the Soviet government statement immediately after it was issued as a "serious warning" to "the expansionists from Tel Aviv." The *Pravda* commentary on the statement omits these phrases. Apparently Brezhnev is less willing than Grechko and certain Russian nationalists to threaten Soviet intervention, even in a highly veiled fashion. This suggests indecision on Brezhnev's part, and less doubt on the part of Grechko and perhaps Polyansky, as to the desirability of a Soviet airlift. Israeli successes on the Golan were probably what changed Brezhnev's mind and resolved this debate.

156. *SR*, Oct. 10, 11, 13, 15, 17, 18, 1973.

157. This interest is expressed in reporting on the reactions of African states and leaders to the war and the Soviet role in it. (*SR*, Oct. 8, 10, 11, 13, 17, 19, 1973.)

158. *Pravda*, Oct. 17, 1973; *SR*, Oct. 17, 1973.

159. *Pravda*, Oct. 17, 1973; *SR*, Oct. 17, 1973.

160. *SR*, Oct. 8, 9, 11, 12, 17, 20, 1973. A very similar image emerges in *Pravda*. It is apparently widely shared among the Soviet elite. (*Pravda*, Oct. 8, 9, 12, 14, 17, 18, 19, 1973.) But attacks on Zionism are noticeably rare in *Izvestiya*. Perhaps they hold little excitement or interest for a managerial and technological audience.

161. Emphasis mine. *SR*, Oct. 8, 1973.

162. *SR*, Oct. 10, 1973. In a report on the proceedings in the UN Security Council after the outbreak of war, *Pravda* and *SR* portray the Egyptian representative as anxious to settle the conflict with Israel. *KZ*'s account of the debate is very similar in other respects, but it omits this passage. (*Pravda*, *SR* and *KZ*, Oct. 10, 1973.)

In welcoming Japanese Premier Tanaka to the USSR at the beginning of the war, Brezhnev delivered a speech which contained an extended reference to the Middle East conflict. All the major Soviet newspapers carried reports of world press reactions to this speech. The reports in *Pravda* and *SR* include the following passage, which is omitted by *KZ*:

"The USSR is prepared to contribute to the implementation of a just and lasting peace in the Middle East. Under such headlines on their front pages Beirut newspapers report the speech of the General Secretary of the Central Committee of the Communist Party of the Soviet Union, citing his statements concerning the situation in the Middle East and the intention of the Soviet Union to devote its efforts to the establishment of a just, lasting peace in the Middle East [and] to the achievement of guaranteed security for all countries and peoples of this region." (*Pravda, SR*, Oct. 10, 1973.)

163. *SR*, Oct. 9, 1973. In reporting world press reaction to the Soviet government statement on the war, *Pravda* and *SR* observe that

"The press of the socialist countries emphasizes that the Soviet government reflects the constructive and realistic position of the USSR on the question of a just political settlement in the Middle East." (*Pravda, SR*, Oct. 9, 1973.)

KZ omits this paragraph, substituting for it a Bulgarian newspaper's comment on the USSR's "international obligation to support the friendly Arab countries." (*KZ*, Oct. 9, 1973.)

164. *SR*, Oct. 11, 12, 16, 24, 1973.

165. *SR* quotes a statement by the Soviet Afro-Asian Solidarity Committee to the effect that the "Israeli aggressors attempt to maintain an explosive situation in the Middle East in order to implement their far-reaching expansionist plans." (Oct. 9, 1973.)

166. *SR* rarely boasts about the Arabs' military performance or the quality of the weapons they have been given, despite the fact that it generally brags a great deal about Soviet achievements and virtues.

167. The title of this article suggests a good deal about *KP*'s political views: "And Again — the Flames of War: From the History of the Crimes of Zionism Against the Arab Peoples," *KP*, Oct. 12, 1973. The article was probably written and sent to print before news of the success of the Israeli counter-offensive on the Golan (Oct. 11) was received and digested in Moscow. By the night of Oct. 11, the

92

Israelis had crossed the 1967 cease-fire lines and were within twenty-five miles of Damascus.

168. I.e., when it must reprint official speeches or documents which themselves mention it (*KP*, Oct. 9, 11, 17, 1973).

It is instructive to campare the Soviet government statement on the war, published by all the major papers and reflecting the views of Brezhnev and Kosygin, with *KP*'s commentary on it. In an article entitled "Statement of Soviet Youth," the youth newspaper in effect gives its own version of the government statement, modifying it in subtle but significant ways. Both statements begin by noting the outbreak of hostilities and the human and material losses resulting from them. But the government statement then goes on to observe that the war brings new dangers to "the peoples of the world," who "greeted the recent process of international detente with relief." The "Statement of Soviet Youth" pointedly omits this passage on detente and its warm reception from the world's peoples. (*Pravda*, Oct. 8, 1973; *KP*, Oct. 9, 1973.)

One might also compare the report on world press reactions to the government statement in *SR* (in comparison to *Pravda* a restrained supporter of detente) with the report which appeared in *Komsomolskaya Pravda*. The *SR* version concludes with the observation

"Many newspapers view the statement of the Soviet governmant as a clear confirmation of the peaceful foreign policy of the USSR and its aspiration to strengthen the trend toward reduction of international tensions."

The *KP* version, otherwise quite similar, does not mention either the peacefulness of Soviet foreign policy or international appreciation of it. (*SR*, Oct. 9, 1973; *KP*, Oct. 9, 1973.)

169. *KP*, Oct. 9, 12, 17, 1973.

170. Like *KZ* and *SR* (and unlike *Pravda*), *KP* supports the interpretation of the Soviet government statement as a "serious warning" from the USSR to the "expansionists" from Tel Aviv." Presumably the warning is "stop fighting and agree to withdraw to your 1967 borders or we shall help the Arabs force you to do so." See note 155.

171. *KP*, Oct. 12, 1973.

172. *KP*, Oct. 9, 10, 11, 14, 17, 18, 20, 21, 1973.

173. *KP*, Oct. 18, 21, 1973.

174. *KP*, Oct. 18, 21, 1973.

175. *KP*, Oct. 18, 21, 1973.

176. *KP*, Oct. 21, 1973.

177. *KP*, Oct. 12, 16, 1973.

178. *KP*, Oct. 13, 14, 16, 1973.

179. *KP*, Oct. 16, 1973.

180. *KP*, Oct. 21, 1973.

181. *KP*, Oct. 17, 21, 1973. A cartoon which appears in *KP* in several variations during the war displays a hook-nosed soldier, the Star of David inscribed on his palm and missiles on each fingernail, emerging from a tank turret dripping with blood. This particular version was printed on Oct. 12, 1973, p. 3. There are more derogatory comments on Zionism and Zionists in *KP* than in any other major Soviet paper (*KP*, Oct. 9, 12, 14, 18, 20, 21, 1973).

182. *KP*, Oct. 14, 1973.

183. *KP*, Oct. 14, 1973.

184. *KP*, Oct. 14, 1973.

185. *KP*, Oct. 14, 1973 (emphasis mine). See also *KP*, Oct. 21, 1973 for another article in this vein by the same author.

186. Like all the major Soviet newspapers, *KP* does publish the text of the Soviet–Japanese statement, issued at the conclusion of Premier Tanaka's visit, which calls on all states to "adhere in relations with one another to the principle of resolution of conflicts by negotiations..." (*KP*, Oct. 11, 1973.) For *Pravda*'s interest in a settlement see *Pravda*, Oct. 7, 8, 9, 10, 11, 13, 21, 22, 1973.

187. *KP*, Oct. 17, 1973.
It is true that, like the Soviet–Japanese statement, Brezhnev's speech welcoming Tanaka is printed in all the major papers, including *KP*. Both these documents indicate Soviet support for a just and lasting peace in the Middle East without mentioning Israel's borders, the Palestinians, or Jewish immigration to Israel. (*KP*, Oct. 9, 11, 1973.) However, one should note that in a subsequent reference to this speech, *KP* distinguishes itself from the other papers by omitting a passage endorsing the Middle East policy which Brezhnev set forth in it. This passage notes that Foreign Minister Gromyko especially emphasized to a visiting delegation of Arab ambassadors the significance of this speech and the fact that Brezhnev
"precisely and clearly expressed the determination of the Soviet Union to continue exerting every effort in the interests of insuring a just and

Pravda also quotes Kissinger as having declared that "our two countries [have] 'substantially reduced the risk of direct conflict between the USSR and the U.S. at crisis points.'" *IZ* and *SR* omit this last sentence from their reports. *KZ* reports other portions of Kissinger's remarks, but omits all of these statements about detente. *KP* and *Trud* do not even mention that the press conference was held. (*Pravda*, Oct. 10, 1973; *IZ*, Oct. 11, 1973; *SR*, Oct. 10, 1973.)

195. *Trud*, Oct. 14, 1973.

196. "To Comrade Brezhnev," *Trud*, Oct. 17, 1973.

197. "Speech By Comrade Shelepin," *Trud*, Oct. 17, 1973. The *Pravda* version of Shelepin's speech omits this paragraph (*Pravda*, Oct. 17, 1973).

198. *Trud*, Oct. 14, 17, 1973.

199. *Trud*, Oct. 14, 17, 1973.

200. *Trud*, Oct. 14, 1973.

201. "Speech By Comrade Shelepin," *Trud*, Oct. 17, 1973. The *Pravda* version omits this sentence (*Pravda*, Oct. 17, 1973).

202. "Speech By Comrade Shelepin," *Trud*, Oct. 17, 1973. The *Pravda* version omits this paragraph (*Pravda*, Oct. 17, 1973).

203. *Trud* gives considerable attention to the role of Soviet weapons and training in the war. It would not do so unless it approved of such projects ((*Trud*, Oct. 11, 12, 13, 14, 16, 17, 1973).

204. *Trud* does print the Soviet-Japanese statement, which contains such a reference (Oct. 11, 1973).

205. This is apparent in the reporting of the Security Council debates. On Oct. 9, for example, the Egyptian representative Zayat addressed himself to the question, on what principles must a political settlement be based. *Pravda* summarizes his remarks in its account of the proceedings. *Trud* carries a report which is otherwise very similar but which does not mention Zayat's statements (*Pravda*, *Trud*, Oct. 10, 1973).

206. The Soviet–Japanese statement does, however, call for such a guarantee (*Trud*, Oct. 11, 1973).

207. Joseph Schumpeter, *Imperialism and Social Classes*, Meridian Books (Cleveland: The World Publishing Company, 1951), pp. 64–98.

208. Roman Kolkowicz, *The Soviet Military and the Communist Party* (Princeton: Princeton University Press, 1967).

209. Tatu, *Power in the Kremlin*, pp. 170–175, 364–428.

lasting peace in the Middle East and providing guaranteed security for all states and peoples of this region.

"The USSR Minister of Foreign Affairs reaffirmed the Soviet Union's determination to continue the consistent implementation of this principled policy." (*Pravda*, Oct. 12, 1973; *KP*, Oct. 12, 1973. Translated in *Current Digest of the Soviet Press*, XXV [Nov. 7, 1973], 9.)

188. *KP* calls attention to these aspects of Soviet–Arab relations even in the absence of peace. (Oct. 12, 1973.)

189. Neither Islam nor Arab nationalism have been easily reconciled with Communism, and both have a strong hold on the loyalties of masses and elites in the Middle East. In many other parts of the Third World, such as sub-Saharan Africa, Latin America, the Asian subcontinent and Southeast Asia, local ideologies tend to be less at variance with Communism or less successful in retaining widespread and deep commitment.

190. *KP*, Oct. 11, 12, 13, 14, 16, 17, 18, 20, 1973.

191. *KP*, Oct. 11, 17, 1973.

192. As head of the Youth Organization, he berated the Komsomols for their poor grounding in Communism and their pursuit of "alien" pastimes like vulgar dancing and abstract art. As KGB Chairman, he tried to enlarge police controls over the activities of writers and artists.

Shelepin participated in an important Soviet delegation to Peking in September, 1959. The Soviet break with China occurred shortly after, and Shelepin opposed Khrushchev's policy on this matter. He also tried to discourage Khrushchev from pursuing detente with the United States.

193. *Trud*, Oct. 14, 1973.

194. On the fourth day of the war, the American Secretary of State held a press conference in which he defended the importance and achievements of detente. The treatment of this event in the Soviet press offers something of a yardstick with which to measure the attitudes of each of the major papers and their backers toward detente — its value and the possibility of achieving it. *Pravda* reports Kissinger as having urged the U.S. and the USSR to "proceed from the concept of peaceful coexistence" in their mutual search for peace,. It observes that Kissinger "noted in this regard 'the successful transformation of U.S.–Soviet relations in many important areas.'"

U.N. CIVILIAN OPERATIONS IN THE CONGO
House, Arthur H., United States Senate
350pp   0-8191-0321-7 $9.45   January, '78
The definitive account of U.N. civilian operations in the Congo.
Focuses on economic, as well as political and diplomatic aspects.

AMERICAN FOREIGN POLICY IN SOUTHERN AFRICA: THE STAKES AND THE
  STANCE
Lemarchard, René, Ed., University of Florida
400pp   0-8191-0324 $9.75   December, '77
Herskovits award winner Lemarchand and his contributors, Larry
Bowman, William Foltz, Allen Isaacman, Edgar Lockwood, Tilden
Lemelle and Hunt Davis, address such issues as corporate influence,
the role of the CIA, the impact of Black Americans and other timely
topics. "...the papers are of uniformly high quality." CHOICE

CZECHOSLOVAKIA'S ROLE IN SOVIET STRATEGY
Josef Kalvoda, Saint Joseph College
391pp   0-8191-0413-2 $9.25   January, '78
"...a thoroughly researched, well-documented, timely and per-
suasive work of lasting value." - Rudolph C. Krempl, Secretary
General, Comenius World Council. "...one of the better books
about contemporary Czechoslovakia." -M.K. Dziewanowski, Pro-
fessor of History, Boston University.

PALESTINIANS WITHOUT PALESTINE: A STUDY OF POLITICAL SOCIALI-
ZATION AMONG PALESTINIAN YOUTHS
Alice and Yasumasa Kuroda, Chaminade University and University
of Hawaii
287pp   0-8191-0479-5 $9.75   February, '78
Based on a recent survey of Palestinian youths, this study ex-
amines the roots of Palestine/Israeli anomosities and offers
helpful suggestions for understanding the political matura-
tion process of the Palestinian young people.

THINKING THE THINKABLE: INVESTMENT IN HUMAN SURVIVAL
Ed., Nish Jamgotch, Jr., University of North Carolina at
Charlotte
360pp   0-8191-0402-7 $9.75   February '78
A collection of nine essays dealing with population, food
shortages, energy depletion, ecological abuse and other global
concerns. Contributors include Robert McNamara, Denis Hayes,
Russell Peterson and Edward Azar.

POLITICS AND ADMINISTRATION IN BRAZIL
Ed., Jean-Claude Garcia-Zamor, Howard University
ca. 450pp   0-8191-0509-0 $12.75   August '78
A collection of articles by Brazilian and American scholars
covering the gamut of political, military and administrative
affairs.

CHICANO POLITICS: A THEORETICAL AND BEHAVIORAL ANALYSIS OF
CHICANOS IN AMERICAN POLITICS
Vigil, Maurilio E., New Mexico Highlands University
375pp.   0-8191-0110 $9.45   January, '77
Employing a conceptual approach, this comprehensive study ex-
amines the political development of the Southwest's most
activist minority group "...libraries interested in strengthening their collections in (American politics and Chicano studies)
should have this volume on their shelves." - CHOICE

THE CHIT'LIN CONTROVERSY: RACE AND PUBLIC POLICY IN AMERICA
Charles P. Henry, Dennison University
Lorenzo Morris, Massachusetts Institute of Technology
157pp   0-8191-0471-X $7.25   February, '78
"...a rare book...I don't think there is anything like it in
the field." - Theodore J. Lowi, Cornell University

INTERPRETERS AND CRITICS OF THE COLD WAR
Kenneth W. Thompson, University of Virginia
ca. 110pp   0-8191-0504-X $5.75   ca. September, '78
An attempt to analyze the views of a group of interpreter
critics who fall neither within the school of revision his-
torians nor of orthodox writers on the cold war.

THE FEDERALIST WITHOUT TEARS
Stearns, Jean, Brandywine College
178pp   0-8191-0106-0 $5.50   January, '77
Twenty six of the most important papers have been rewritten in
contemporary language. A unique sourcebook for high school and
undergraduate history and political science courses.

POLICY-MAKING IN THE AMERICAN SYSTEM: THE CASE OF THE MANPOWER,
DEVELOPMENT AND TRAINING PROGRAM
George T. Menake, Montclair State College of New Jersey
387pp   0-8191-0409-4 $10.50   January, '78
A study of American policy-making in the area of social welfare
legislation.

THE PRESIDENCY AND THE MASS MEDIA IN THE AGE OF TELEVISION
William C. Spragens, Bowling Green State University
428pp   0-8191-0476-0 $10.75   February, '78
The author, a former newsman, traces the development of the
relationship between the White House and the Washington correspondent corps since 1945 and offers valuable insights into the
nature of this very important interplay.